Readings for Art, Culture and Society

Edited by

EUNG-SOON WON
JONG HUH
KEON-SOO LEE
MYOUNG-AH SHIN
HAN-GYU LEE
JAE-HAK YOON

SHINASA

Readings for Art, Culture and Society

SHINASA Publishing Co.
349-6 (B/D 602) Gil-Dong, Kangdong-Ku,
Seoul, Korea
Registered: 9-52 (January 5, 1956)
Tel: (02) 474-4511
Fax: (02) 474-4106
E-mail: shinasa@chollian.net
Homepage: www.shinasa.co.kr

First published 2001

Price: ₩ 10,000

ISBN: 89-8396-155-4 93740

Contents

Section Ⅰ: Literature

Section Ⅱ: Culture

Section Ⅲ: Society, Politics and Science

Section Ⅳ: Women

Section I : Literature

THE PLEASURE OF WRITING

Alan Alexander Milne **(1882-1956)**

English Humorist, the originator of the immensely popular stories of Christopher Robin and his toy bear, Winnie-the-Pooh.

Works: *Winnie-the-Pooh* (1926). *The Hours at Pooh Corner* (1928)

Sometimes when the printer is waiting for an article which really should have been sent to him the day before, I sit at my desk and wonder if there is any possible subject in the whole world upon which I can possibly find anything to say. On one such occasion I left it to Fate, which decided, by means of a dictionary opened at random, that I should deliver myself of a few thoughts about goldfish. (You will find this article later on in the book.) But today I do not need to bother about a subject. Today I am without a care. Nothing less has happened than that I have a new nib in my pen.

In the ordinary way, when Shakespeare writes a tragedy, or Mr. Blank gives you one of his charming little essays, a certain amount of thought goes on before pen is put to paper. One cannot write "Scene I. An Open Place. Thunder and Lightning. Enter Three Witches," or "As I look up from my window, the nodding daffodils beckon to me to take the morning," one cannot give of one's best in this way on the spur of the moment. At least, others cannot. But when I have a new nib in my pen, then I can go straight from my breakfast to the blotting-paper, and a new sheet of foolscap fills itself magically with a stream of blue-black words. When poets and idiots talk of the pleasure of writing, they mean the pleasure of giving a piece of their minds to the public; with an old nib a tedious business. They do not mean (as I do) the pleasure of the artist in seeing beautifully shaped "k's" and sinuous "s's" grow beneath his steel. Anybody else writing this article might wonder "Will my readers like it?" I only tell myself "How the compositors will love it!"

But perhaps they will not love it. Maybe I am a little above their heads. I remember on one First of January receiving an anonymous postcard wishing me a happy New Year, and suggesting that I should give the compositors a happy New Year also by writing more generously. In those days I got a thousand words upon one sheet 8 in. by 5 in. I adopted the suggestion, but it was a wrench; as it would be for a painter of miniatures forced to spend the rest of his life painting the Town Council of Boffington in the manner of Herkomer. My canvases are bigger now, but they are still impressionistic. "Pretty, but what is it?" remains the obvious comment; one steps back a pace and saws the air with the hand; "You see it better from here, my love," one says to one's wife. But if there be one compositor not carried away by the mad rush of life, who in a leisurely hour (the luncheon one, for instance) looks at the beautiful words with the eye of an artist, not of a wage earner, he, I think, will be satisfied; he will be as glad as I am of my new nib. Does it matter, then, what you who see only the printed word think of it?

A woman, who had studied what she called the science of calligraphy, once offered to tell my character from my handwriting. I prepared a special sample for her; it was full of sentences like "To be good is to be happy," "Faith is the lode-star of life," "We should always be kind to animals," and so on. I wanted her to do her best. She gave the morning to it, and told me at lunch that I was "synthetic." Probably you think that the compositor has failed me here and printed "synthetic" when I wrote "sympathetic." In just this way I misunderstood my calligraphist at first, and I looked as sympathetic as I could. However, she repeated "synthetic" so that there could be no mistake. I begged her to tell me more, for I had thought that every letter would reveal a secret, but all she would add was "and not analytic." I went about for the rest of the day saying proudly to myself "I am synthetic! I am synthetic! I am synthetic!" and then I would add regretfully, "Alas, I am not analytic!" I had no idea what it meant.

And how do you think she had deduced my syntheticness? Simply from the fact that, to save time, I join some of my words together. That isn't being synthetic, it is being in a hurry. What she should have said was, "You are a busy man; your life is one constant whirl; and probably you are of excellent moral character and kind to animals." Then one would feel that one did not write in vain.

My pen is getting tired; it has lost its first fair youth. However, I can still go on. I was at school with a boy whose uncle made nibs. If you detect traces of erudition in this article, of which any decent man might be expected to be innocent, I owe it to that boy.

He once told me how many nibs his uncle made in a year; luckily I have forgotten. Thousands, probably. Every term that boy came back with a hundred of them; one expected him to be very busy. After all, if you haven't the brains or the inclination to work, it is something to have the nibs. These nibs, however, were put to better uses. There is a game you can play with them; you flick your nib against the other boy's nib, and if a lucky shot puts the head of yours under his, then a sharp tap capsizes him, and you have a hundred and one in your collection, There is a good deal of strategy in the game (whose finer points I have now forgotten), and I have no doubt that they play it at the Admiralty in the off season. Another game was to put a clean nib in your pen, place it lightly against the cheek of a boy whose head was turned away from you, and then call him suddenly. As Kipling says, we are the only really humorous race. This boy's uncle died a year or two later and left about £80,000, but none of it to his nephew. Of course, he had had the nibs every term. One mustn't forget that.

The nib I write this with is called the "Canadian Quill"; made, I suppose, from some steel goose which flourished across the seas, and which Canadian housewives have to explain to their husbands every Michaelmas. Well, it has seen me to the end of what I wanted to say — if indeed I wanted to say anything. For it was enough for me this morning just to write; with spring coming in through the open windows and my good Canadian quill in my hand, I could have copied out a directory. That is the real pleasure of writing.

FAREWELL TO TOBACCO

Robert S. Lynd **(1892-1970)**

Along with Helen M. Lynd (1897-1982), he wrote *Middletown* (1929), a classic sociological study of an American city. The community called Middletown was actually Muncie, Indiana. This study was among the first that demonstrated the discrepancy between American egalitarian beliefs and the class structure of an American community. It also focused on the conflict between the ideological emphasis on individualism and free enterprise and the demands created by the entry of this city into an industrialized and highly organized economy.

Boswell told Dr. Johnson that Steele published his *Christian Hero* 'with the avowed purpose of obliging himself to lead a religious life.' It is evidence of a touching faith in the power of the printed word that Steele should have thought that he had only to commit himself to a better life on paper in order to be forced into leading it for the rest of his days. Or, perhaps, he may have reasoned more subtly than this. He may have said to himself : 'I will write such a book that, as the author, I shall be unable to fall from grace without exciting universal ridicule'; and, having failed to keep upright by any other means, he hoped to terrorize himself into doing so by creating a situation in which he could not slip without becoming the butt of every fool. The experiment, it is to be feared, was not a success, and for two centuries fools and wise men have smiled though without malice at stories of the Christian hero in his cups. 'Steele, I believe,' said Dr. Johnson, 'practised the lighter vices.' Steele himself, it is said, was bitterly offended by the way in which his fellow-officers subjected 'the least levity' in his words or actions to criticism as being incongruous in the author of *The Christian Hero*. The publication of his treatise, evidently, brought him not the piety he hoped but the ridicule he feared. With such a warning from the past it seems madness in any writer who is not a saint to commit himself in public to a life of virtue. I have at times been timid of praising virtue even in other people lest I should afterwards seem a humbug measured by a standard that I had rallied to at least in words. And yet, like Steele, I am tempted at times to commit myself publicly — to commit myself publicly, say, to one of the lighter virtues so that I may know that I cannot become a backslider — strange word! — without also becoming an object of derision to my friends.

Today, for example, I wish to give up tobacco. I do not mean that I wish to give it up as other men do, but to give it up finally. I have given it up as other men do again and again. I have trifled with abstinence for a lunar month at a time. If at the end of the month I yielded to temptation, however, I did not feel humiliated in the company of my fellowmortals. I was merely amused, and regarded my lapse as a checkmate that must sooner or later have brought the game to an end. I am not sure that I did not even like myself a little better for having made a concession to the weakness of human nature. All men idealize themselves, and in the mirror of self-satisfaction weakness of will seems an unusually attractive form of good humour. I do not know how in the world men are ever to become virtuous if they remain so fatuously in love with themselves as they make it up with their sins. I should like to be able to say good-bye to tobacco in such a way that, if ever I reverted to it, I should feel so ashamed that I should have to leave Europe and begin life over again in the colonies under an assumed name. When I sat down to write this morning, it was in the hope that I might be able to utter a good-bye so terrible that tobacconists would grow pale when I walked past the doors of their shops. But how can I? Smoking, I am convinced, is for me a vice, because I cannot smoke without smoking to excess. But I cannot regard it as a vice in other people, so that it is difficult to denounce tobocco as a weed in the Devil's garden. If I could only hate it as Ruskin hated it, I might be able to write a new version of *The Christian Hero*, depicting a man who was too proud to smoke. But how can I hate tobacco when I think of all the pleasures with which it has been associated ever since I can remember? I grew up in the smell of it — pipe-smoke in my father's study and snuff in the nursery. My nurse was a good-natured Christian widow who every Saturday night went off in her jet-black bonnet and beaded cape to see her daughter, and who always brought back a little bag of pear or acid drops for me, and for herself a little bag of snuff shaped like the horn of plenty. She usually left the snuff on the corner of the mantelpiece, whence it overflowed, as it were, and permeated the room with the smell of a pleasant kind of pepper. How often have I sat on her knee, listening to the tale of the last agonies of the Protestant martyrs and sneezing where less fortunate children would have wept! How any one can regard snufftaking as a disgusting habit I have never since been able to understand. I associate it myself with the infinite kindness of a woman who would never admit that anything that I did was wrong and to whom I was so devoted that I remember arguing doggedly with my father that the correct pronunciation of 'teaspoon' was 'tayspun' and that 'bread' should be pronounced 'braid.' It was with the smell of snuff in my infant nostrils that I first learned to admire a heroism that I have never been able to emulate, as I listened to stories of the relief of Kandahar and of the slave war in America (in both of which relatives of hers had taken part) and enjoyed at times the back-straightening happiness of having a soldier's medal pinned to my breast. It was in a cloud of snuff that I first heard of King William and the Battle of the Boyne and was inducted into music with 'The Protestant Boys', 'Dare to be a Daniel', 'Ye Banks and Braes' and 'Old Dog Tray'. In later years, when I became a journalist, I tried to acquire a taste for snuff myself, for the printers in the case-room in Manchester were constantly holding out a hospitable snuff-box. On one occasion I even took to it as a means of giving up smoking, but a printer warned me that it was a still more enslaving habit. 'I have seen myself,' he said, 'getting up out of bed in the middle of the night for a pinch of snuff.' I suggested that at least it had not such a bad effect on the health as smoking.

'I have seen,' he replied, 'a compositor falling on the floor in a fit in Manchester, and *he* was a great snuff-taker.' It is lamentable that, just when you have at last discovered what seems a perfectly innocent habit, someone invariably comes along with a raven's warning. It is almost impossible to become virtuous, indeed, merely by changing one's vice.

As for smoking, how can any one even regard it as a vice? It was only after years of thought about the matter that I was able to persuade myself that abstinence from tobacco was not a defect of manhood in a grown-up man. To have abolished tobacco would have seemed in my first years like banishing the clouds from the summer sky. There are two sights of which I never grew tired as a child — the sight of tobacco smoke issuing from a man's mouth and the sight of a man shaving. How like Zeus in an arm-chair a man appears with those fragrant clouds about his head! How delightful it is in his absence for a child to take down his pipes and look at them — the crooked briar, and the long straight clay with the white hand embossed on the bowl — and to open the tobacco jar and smell the most delicious of the herbs! Alas, it is impossible to admire such things for long without desiring to produce those magical clouds oneself and to taste the sweetness of that honeydew, as all tobacco seemed to be called in those days. I cannot have been more than five years old when, finding myself alone in the study, I made the great experiment. I remember, after a few minutes of it, creeping away to die in the hollow under the desk, flanked on each side by drawers full of sermons. I needed no sermons just then any more than the damned, and, indeed, I got none when I was discovered and carried gently to bed. There may be men who would have forsworn tobacco after such an experience, but, though I did not attempt a pipe again for a year or two, I was already a slave to the idea of smoking, and, even while I was still attending a dame's school, I used often to go into a spirit grocery on the way home and buy cinnamon cigarettes with another boy, which we smoked among the flower-beds and the glass frames in a nursery man's garden. We frequently discussed whether it was wrong, for we both had consciences, but we decided without difficulty that, as cinnamon was not tobacco, to smoke cinnamon cigarettes was not smoking. 'This is sappy good,' the boy would say as he puffed at his cigarette. 'Put your hand there' — and he would point to a waistcoat button — 'and I'll show you the smoke coming out of my eyes.' But, if you did what he said, he would suddenly bring the lighted end of his cigarettes down on your hand, and two young smokers would find themselves tussling on the box-bordered path. I have heard of other boys smoking such things as tea and brown paper, but I remained faithful to cinnamon until I was old enough to smoke tobacco. Duke's Cameo cigarettes — you remember the little boxes, each containing the picture of a Parisian dancer or a statuette — are there any cigarettes like them nowadays? They had only one drawback: they left a smell of tobacco on the breath. I used, on reaching home after smoking them, to make stealthily for the pantry and to drink a large draught of milk, little though I liked it, in the hope that a smell of milk might deceive members of the family. I was conceived that the smell of cachous merely gave one away, and I had not the desperate courage of a fellow-schoolboy who used to chew the heads of matches and soap for the purpose of sparing his mother the knowledge that he was a smoker. What kind of drug-fiend she must have thought him, I cannot imagine; but it is a miracle that he did not die untimely of phossy-jaw. Even when we had taken to real tobacco, however, we did not at first smoke very much except during the holidays, and I should not describe myself as having been a regular smoker until the age of sixteen. By that time I smoked a pipe and one ounce of tobacco a week — Log Cabin or Pioneer or Tortoiseshell — which I always bought at the same shop from a very tall and beautifully-dressed lady whose trembling slave I was. I thought she was like a Spaniard, for she had glorious black hair and glorious red lips and glorious white teeth when she smiled. I liked her to be alone in the shop when I went in. I always meant to talk to her. But somehow I never could say anything but 'An ounce of Log Cabin, please,' and then 'Thank you' as I took off my cap and went out. Thus I have also an association of love with tobacco. …But, if I were to tell you all the associations I have with tobacco, I should find myself writing an autobiography in ten volumes, for, save for a few brief periods of austerity, I have been smoking continuously ever since. That is why I am now so eager to say farewell to tobacco — to say such a farewell as will do no dishonour to a herb that has given me so much pleasure and at the same time will commit me to treating it with heartless indifference for the rest of my days. I doubt if Einstein himself could solve such a problem. All the same, I will try. Steep and difficult is the hill of virtue, and on the distant summit of it I descry the tiny figure of a man who does not smoke.

THE LUNCHEON

W. Somerset Maugham (1874-1965)

British novelist, playwright, short-story writer, highest paid author in the world in the 1930s. Despite his popularity, Maugham did not gain serious recognition.

Works: *Of Human Bandage* (1915), *The Moon and Six Pence* (1917), *The Summing Up* (1938)

I caught sight of her at the play and in answer to her beckoning. I went over during the interval and sat down beside her. It was long since I had last seen her and if someone had not mentioned her name I hardly think I would have recognized her. She addressed me brightly.

"Well, it's many years since we first met. How time does fly! We're none of us getting any younger. Do you remember the first time I saw you? You asked me to luncheon."

Did I remember?

It was twenty years ago and I was living in Paris. I had a tiny apartment in the Latin quarter overlooking a cemetery and I was earning barely enough money to keep body and soul together. She had read a book of mine and had written to me about it. I answered, thanking her and presently I received from her another letter saying that she was passing through Paris and would like to have a chat with me; but her time was limited and the only free moment she had was on the following Thursday; she was spending the morning at the Luxemburg and would I give her a little luncheon at Foyot's afterwards? Foyot's is a restaurant at which the French senators eat and it was so far beyond my means that I had never even thought of going there. But I was flattered and I was too young to have learned to say no to a woman. (For men, I may add, learn this until they are too old to make if on any consequence to a woman what they say.) I had eighty francs (gold francs) to last me the rest of the month and a modest luncheon should not cost more than fifteen. If I cut out coffee for the next two weeks I could manage well enough.

I answered that I would meet my friend — by correspondence — at Foyot's on Thursday at half-past twelve. She was not so young as I expected and in appearance imposing rather than attractive. She was in fact a woman of forty (a charming age, but not one that excites a sudden and devastating passion at first sight, and gave me the impression of having more teeth, white and large and even, than were necessary for any practical purpose. She was talkative, but since she seemed inclined to talk about me I was prepared to be an attentive listener.

I was startled when the bill of fare was brought, for the prices were a great deal higher than I had anticipated. But she reassured me.

"Oh, don't say that," I answered generously.

"I never eat more than one thing. I think people eat far too much nowadays. A little fish, perhaps. I wonder if they have any salmon."

Well, it was early in the year for salmon and it was not on the bill of fare, but I asked the waiter if there was any. Yes, a beautiful salmon had just come in, it was the first they had had. I ordered it for my guest. The waiter asked her if she would have something while it was being cooked.

"No" she answered, "I never eat more than one thing. Unless you had a little caviare. I never mind caviare."

My heart sank a little. I knew I could not afford caviare, but I could not very well tell her that. I told the waiter by all means to bring caviare. For myself I chose the cheapest dish on the menu and that was a mutton chop.

"I think you're unwise to eat meat," she said. "I don't know how you can expect to work after eating heavy things like chops. I don't believe in overloading my stomach."

Then came the question of drink.

"I never drink anything for luncheon," she said.

"Neither do I," I answered promptly.

"Except white wine," she proceeded as though I had not spoken. "These French white wines are so light. They're wonderful for the digestion."

"What would you like?" I asked, hospitable still, but not exactly effusive.

She gave me a bright and amicable flash of her white teeth.

"My doctor won't let me drink anything but champagne."

I fancy I turned a trifle pale. I ordered half a bottle. I mentioned casually that my doctor had absolutely forbidden me to drink champagne.

"What are you going to drink then?"

"Water."

She ate the caviare and she ate salmon. She talked gaily of art and literature and music. But I wondered what the bill would come to.

When my mutton chop arrived she took me quite seriously to task. "I see that you're in the habit of eating a heavy luncheon. I'm sure it's mistake. Why don't you follow my example and just eat one thing? I'm sure you'd feel ever so much better for it."

"I'm only going to eat one thing," I said, as the waiter came again with the bill of fare.

She waved him aside with an airy gesture.

"No, no, I never eat anything for luncheon, Just a bite, I never want more than that, and I eat that more as an excuse for conversation than anything else. I couldn't possibly eat anything more unless they had some of those giant asparagus. I should be sorry to leave Paris without having some of them."

My heart sank. I had seen them in the shops and I knew that they were horribly expensive. My mouth had often watered at the sight of them.

"Madame wants to know if you have any of those giant asparagus," I asked the waiter.

I tried with all my might to will him to say no. A happy smile spread over his broad, priestlike face, and he assured me that they had some so large, so splendid, so tender, that it was marvel.

"I'm not in the least hungry," my guest sighed, "but if you insist I don't mind having some asparagus."

I ordered them.

"Aren't you going to have any?"

"No, I never eat asparagus."

"I know there are people who don't like them. The fact is, you ruin your palate by all the meat you eat."

We waited for the asparagus to be cooked. Panic seized me. It was not a question now how much money I should have left over for the rest of the month, but whether I had enough to pay the bill. It would be mortifying to find myself ten francs short and be obliged to borrow from my guest. I could not bring myself to do that. I knew exactly how much I had and if the bill came to more I made up my mind that I would put my hand in my pocket and with a dramatic cry start up and say it had been picked. Of course it would be awkward if she had not money enough either to pay the bill. Then the only thing would be to leave my watch and say I would come back and pay later.

The asparagus appeared. They were enormous, succulent and appetising. The smell of the melted butter tickled my nostrils as the nostrils of Jehovah were tickled by the burned offerings of the virtuous Semites. I watched the abandoned woman thrust them down her throat in large voluptuous mouthfuls and in my polite way I discoursed on the condition of the drama in the Balkans.

At last she finished.

"Coffee?" I said.

"Yes, just an ice cream and coffee." she answered.

I was past caring now, so I ordered coffee for myself and an ice cream and coffee for her.

"You know, there's one thing. I thoroughly believe in," she said, as she ate the ice cream.

"One should always get up from a meal feeling one could eat a little more."

"Are you still hungry?" I asked faintly.

"Oh, no, I'm not hungry; I don't eat luncheon. I have a cup of coffee in the morning and then dinner, but I never eat more than one thing for luncheon. I was speaking for you."

"Oh, I see!"

Then a terrible thing happened. While we were waiting for the coffee, the headwaiter, with an ingratiating smile on his false face, came up to us bearing a large basket full of huge peaches.

LIKES AND DISLIKES

James Agate **(1877-1947)**

English drama critic. Agate wrote for *the Manchester Guardian,* serving as its theatre critic from 1907 to 1914. For the last twenty-four years of his life, he was drama critic for the *London Sunday Times.* He developed a large and faithful following, inspired largely by the obvious enthusiasm he communicated about the theatre and theatre people. His autobiographical diaries, collectively entitled *Ego,* were published in nine volumes (1935-48).

These are my likings.

An old park in our middle England, dripping trees undergrowth, decay, a lady many years disconsolate: bleak pinches, moors and winding roads; old inns, coffee rooms, and faded prints; high noon in market squares, the roguery of dealers, Hodge's reverence to parson and bank manager; all that England which lies between Hogarth and Trollope; the placidity which is content with Rydal Water and the glory of Wordsworth; the eaves and the thatches of Hertfordshire; Surrey's imitation of Corot; the apple-sense of Somerset; the mothy coombes of Devon.

And then the reflex sentimentality of those direct emotions and the play Stevenson would have made of them; the Wardour Street glamour of such words as 'sundial' and 'curfew', the Victorian lilt and cadence of that perfect *raser* King Arthur; the saturated melancholy of headstones. The sentimentality of parchments; old brocades, fans that have not fluttered and lace that has not stirred for a generation; the *mouches* and petulance of *petites marquises*; the painter's sense of great ladies.

I could tease myself that these emotions are so general as not to be worth setting down, were it not that strong affection loses nothing by being shared with the whole world. Sealing wax and sailing ships fascinate me none the less for having appealed to another. Yet there are certain intimate appreciations, discoveries of one's own, to be hugged exultingly. Such the homely lilt of ballads, the crinolined grace of *She Wore a Wreath of Roses*, the faded propriety of *My Mother Bids me Bind my Hair*. I sometimes think they have missed the better half of life who do not know *Claribel*, stern mistress of our tender youth, inexorable guide to wayward fingers. Well do I remember the tone of ivory keys deepening through saffron to rich brown, the nubbly, polished ebonies, the puckered rose-coloured silk lining, the fretted walnut front, the fantastic scroll-work of the maker's name. Collard and Collard — how many hours did my childish soul ponder over all the possible combinations of father and son, uncle and nephew, brothers it may be. I often find myself wondering what has become of the old piano over which half my childhood was wept away. I believe I should know it again by its fragrance, the fragrance of my mother's fingers. As I write the perfume steals across me.

I adore all acting, all masks and subterfuges, all cloaks and garbs of respectability, the obsequiousness of head waiters and the civility of underlings, all rogues and vagabonds soever, the leer of the pavement and the wit of the gutter. I love Bond Street at eleven in the morning, Scott's at noon, some *matineé* at which there shall be question of faded emotion — say, the old retainer's. And then sunset, red as a guardsman's tunic, gilding the front of the westward-going bus, a music-hall, enough money in my pocket to pay the small-hours' supper bill, the lights extinguished and by the butt of a glowing cigar, a last florin for its fellow, a last sixpence for human *débris* insistent with pitiful whine. I love the mystery and peril of the streets. I love to lie lazily in London, to loop my curtains and surrender myself to the hypnotic effect of the one hundred and sixty-three stags and two thousand two hundred and eighty-two hounds in full cry which I must presume to have been my landlord's taste in wallpaper some lustre ago. I like to gaze at framed elevens and fifteens, at the jumbles of racquets and clubs, the jowl of prize-fighter, Vardon at the top of his swing, Miss Letty Lind ineffably in some Chinese fantasy. I like to look down on Regent Street — my rooms are at the top of a nest of actor's clubs, registry offices, shady money-lenders, and still shadier solicitors — and watch the late last loiterer. I love to lie and think of the world as my own, my very own, in which, though I earn a living by rule and in tune with the common whim, I may by the grace of God think what I like and choose the friends who shall make me laugh and the books which shall make me cry. Every man leads a double life in this most precious of senses. In this world of my own I am supreme lord and master, and may shatter and rebuild according to my proper desire. Events in the tangible universe do not as events interest me at all. Kings may die, and empires fade away, but until these happenings are presented in some saturated phrase my consciousness is unaffected. A new planet is of less moment to me than a new reading of an old line. It needed the Shakespearean echo of some journalist's 'Now is England to be tested to her marrow' to move me to the full responsibility of our pledge to Belgium.

I love the vanity of artists stretching their sad fastidiousness on the rack till perfection be found; the martyr's egotism which will sacrifice health and life itself, not that we may read, but that he may write. So the pride of the soldier, caring less for the cause than that he shall die worthily. I love words for their own sake. I love the words 'hyacinth', 'narcissus', 'daffodil', 'dog-rose'; their very look on the page enchants me; they smell more sweetly in the writer's garden than in Nature's rank parterre. I have never seen a trumpet-orchid, yet I know that when I read:

Fly forward, O my heart, from the Foreland to the Start —
We're steaming all too slow,
And it's twenty thousand mile to our little lazy isle
Where the trumpet-orchids blow,

the word conjures up the nostalgia of far-off seas. I love the tinkle of 'onyx', 'chalcedony', 'beryl', more than the trumpery gauds themselves. I love the word 'must-stained' without desire to gaze upon the feet of the treader of grapes; the words 'spikenard' and 'alabaster' without longing for pot or jar. I am crazy for 'jasmine' and for 'jade', and were I a French writer you would find *jadis* on every page. I would give the million I do not possess to flaunt a scutcheon with the device *Désormais*! But if I am in love with words, it must not be supposed that I have no affection for the idea also. Though I would insist that the idea shall emerge from the foam and tumble of its wrappings glorious as any goddess from the sea, yet do I not disdain to disentangle the writer from his own enmeshings, to lie in wait for him, to detect him in his style. I like to hear in the slipshod cadence of Dickens the beating of his great untidy heart; to trace in the lowering of beautiful words to unromantic purpose the infinite common sense of his latter-day successor; to nose the corruption of the decadent in the paint and powder of his prose. Words for me are not the grace-notes of existence, but the very stuff and texture of life. This may be madness, but it is an honest frenzy, and remember that in your own kingdom you have a right to be mad. I like to think of Piccadilly as it must have been in those early days which saw me mewed up in our provinces of sterling worth. Of the *coudoiement* of notabilities. Of the days when Ellen Terry brought a new morning to the jaded world and Irving sent us shuddering to bed; when, touchingly, at eleven-thirty, Mr and Mrs Kendal would make it up again. When Mr Beerbohm Tree was a rising actor and Mr George confesses he was young. When those tremendous initials G. B. S. first growled and thundered in the pages of *The Saturday Review*, Wilde had not tired of confounding peacockery with prose, and the giant Wells was stirring in his sleep. When Rudyard Kipling was a power in the land, Lord Rosebery a Liberal-Imperialist hope, and it seemed as though the Prince would never be king.

I am a good lover, but an even better hater. I have an unparalleled zest for the most moderate of dislikes. I mislike — to put it no more strongly — a great many women and nearly all men, with a special aversion for the type of man adored by women, mincing-mouthed, luxuriant-polled *genre coiffeur*. I mislike the purist who claims that one language should be enough for any writer and secretly begrudges Caesar his dying Latinism; and I mislike all those honest folk who insist upon taking you at the foot of the letter instead of at the top, or at least half-way down. I dislike all aldermen, mayors, beadles, janitors, pew-openers, the whole bag of officialdom; all sham repentances and most sincere ones; all those to whom the night brings counsel, the *oncle à succession*, and the pliant inheritor; the little ninny who insists that the *Moonlight Sonata* is by Mendelssohn. I have a contempt for the Christian who looks down upon the Jew, the white man who animadverts against the black. I have a horror of the Freemason in his cups; of the players of solo-whist; of the actor with pretensions towards edification claiming to raddle his face that ultimately fewer women may raddle theirs, who 'asks a blessing' on his Hamlet. I hate the commonplaces of the train, the street, and the market. I abhor the belly of the sucessful man and the swelling paunch of the Justice. But my particular loathing is reserved for the unknowledgeable fool who says in his heart: 'These things are not within my experience; therefore they cannot be true.'

What a plague is *ennui!* To have been everywhere, seen everything, done everything, to have used up the senses and let slip the supreme boon, is of all moral diseases the last incurable. To be tired of oneself and one's proficiencies, of the feel of a cue, the whip of a club, the way the racquet comes up in the hand, the touch of reins, the 'handle' of your favourite book, all this is indeed to find the world flat and unprofitable. Nothing remains, says your quack, but to take his pills. Nothing remains but to follow my system of exercise, declares some frock-coated Hercules.

There is, we have often been told, valour and to spare in the spirit's triumph over the flesh. But there is ignominy, I take it, in a romantic spleen giving way to massage, in a fine frenzy of melancholy yielding before a system of exercises. I know nothing more humiliating than this o'ercrowing of the spirit by the body. Hamlet himself had done less girding at the world if he had not been, as Gertrude remarks, in poor condition. That the world is out of joint is an old cry. It belongs to our day to advertise all that loss of figure and excess of flesh, baldness and superfluous hair, tuberculosis, which are our inheritance. I have never been able to fathom the delicate arts' survival of these natural shocks. Greatly in their favour has been the lateness of the world's discovery of electricity, X-rays, Swedish drills, and physical exercises. A Musset the picture of rude health, a Chopin who should dedicate a nocturne to Mr Sandow, a Shelley *pére de famille*, a Baudelaire who should be an inside right to be reckoned with — these were unthinkable.

But it is no part of the story-teller's business to argue, especially when he is not too sure of his case, and you could shatter mine by citing the admirable boxer who is responsible for *Pelléas and Mélisande*.

What I am driving at is that life is never as exquisite nor as tragic as it appears on the surface. I am plagued with the keen appreciation of the tendency of things to find their own level, and I see the world through common-sense spectacles. With me the exquisite moment is of short duration; subsidence is always at hand. Grief is tragic, but its expression, except in the hands of the trained actor, grotesque. A woman in tears is the most monstrous of spectacles, birth as lamentable as death, the terror of many an honest execution marred by the vulgarity of the hangman and our vision of the glass which is to refresh him. What, we ask, remains, for the fellow in the evening of his days save the decline to some bar-parlour? Life is always taking the edge off things, and it is become the fashion to scoff at the monster and the grand *détraqué*. One laughs them out of existence, poor souls. Life is reasonable and sane; your true realist should have nothing to do with *bravura*. Life is exactly like a common-sensical novel by — never mind whom, and I fear sometimes lest the Ultimate Cause be made after that author's image. And yet the most modern writers have their cowardices. Which of them dares portray a murderer *bored* with the imbecile chunnerings, the senile irrelevancies of his judge? Which of them will attribute the clear eye and healthy appetite of the released convict less to the joy of freedom than to a *régime* of regular hours and enforced abstinences? They are afraid of their readers, and rightly. What reader would tolerate that I should set down my real feelings on nearing discharge? From me is expected relief from the intermittent panic, the perpetual dread, the nameless horror, whereas all I have to tell is of escape from an ecstasy of boredom. The truth is that even fear cannot endure for ever; the human mechanism has its limits. Soldiers have told of the power at the long last to put fear behind, not that desperate fear which is the moment of valour's catch in the throat, but the more serious dread, the dull foreboding of inaction. Man cannot keep his mind for ever on the rack; God is to be thanked that we have not complete control of our mentality. I have to reason myself to consciousness of the great deeds which are afoot; I have come to feel intuitively that death is cheapening and that it has become a little thing to die.

A little thing in one sense, how tremendous in another! My reverence for the common soldier exceeds all bounds. Even more vital than the compulsion to mete out to hellish torturers the measure they meted out to their helpless victims is the obligation of this country to see no common soldier who has served in France shall ever know the meaning of want. It is for the nation to adopt its cripples and its maimed, to exact from the poor man his contribution of work and from the rich man even to one hundred per cent of that which he hath, rather than that a single one of these unmurmuring brave should starve. Yesterday a man died in my ward whom in ordinary times one would have dismissed as a drunkard and a lecher. I am not content with these old classifications; I am not content with the future life for this soldier which shall be all Michael Angelo and Sebastian Bach. There must be a paradise for the simpletons as for the picked spirits. I am not content with a roll-call of the illustrious dead who shall arise to greet the coming of our latter-day heroes — great Edward and great Harry, the swinging Elizabethan blade, businesslike Roundhead and inefficient Cavalier. Marlborough, Wellington, Napier, Nicholson, Havelock, Gordon — the shining list does not suffice. I am not content though Nelson return a million-fold the kiss he received from Hardy. I want a Valhalla which shall not be a palace, but a home. I think I could trust Lamb to make a sufficient welcome, though it is to Falstaff I should look to discourse of honour in a strain bearable to soldier ears. Nectar and ambrosia may be good taking, but there must be a familiar grog and laughter and good-fellowship. I want a heaven in which horses shall be run, and the laying of odds allowed a sinless occupation. I want to see Sayers and Heenan fight it out again, to roar at Dan Leno, to watch old Grace till the shadows grow long.

The most bizarre conceptions assail me. I do not despair of finding a good terrier, a sufficiency of rats, and an unoccupied corner of the marble floor. I want not only the best the celestial architects may contrive in the way of saloons, but I want the atmosphere of bar-parlours; I want pipes of clay and pint-pots of jasper, common briars and spittoons of jade. Out of doors, playing-fields with well-matched teams, keen-eyed umpires, hysterical supporters, and tapering goal-posts — chrysoprase if you insist, but common deal will do — and a feeling that once a week it will be Saturday afternoon.

I remember reading in some exquisite diary of the War this letter of a soldier:

> Dear Mum, and Dad, and Loving Sisters, Rose, Mabel, and our Gladys,
> I am very pleased to write you another welcome letter as this leaves me at present. Dear Mum and Dad and loving sisters, keep the homes-fires burning. Not arf! The boys are in the pink. Not arf! Dear loving sisters, Rose, Marbel, and our Gladys, keep merry and bright. Not arf!

I place this amongst the most pathetic and most beautiful of the world's letters. It brings tears, and the refrain 'Rose, Mabel, and our Gladys' has the plaintiveness of a litany.

I want a heaven for this writer that shall please him.

Recollections of Childhood

Richard Steele **(1672-1729)**

Irish-born English playwright and essayist, known for his writing in the periodicals *The Tatler* and *The Spectator* in association with Joseph Addison. Steele took the initiative in the founding of these two journalistic enterprises, serving as the first editor of *The Tatler* under the name of Isaac Bickerstaff, and contributing the majority of the essays published in *The Tatler.* Other works by Steele include *The Christian Hero* (1701), an attack on dueling published as a pamphlet, and several plays.

There are those among mankind, who can enjoy no relish of their being, except the world is made acquainted with all that relates to them, and think everything lost that passes unobserved; but others find a solid delight in stealing by the crowd, and modelling their life after such a manner, as is as much above the approbation as the practice of the vulgar. Life being too short to give instances great enough of true friendship or good will, some sages have thought it pious to preserve a certain reverence for the names of their deceased friends; and have withdrawn themselves from the rest of the world at certain seasons, to commemorate in their own thoughts such of their acquaintance who have gone before them out of this life. And indeed, when we are advanced in years, there is not a more pleasing entertainment, than to recollect in a gloomy moment the many we have parted with, that have been dear and agreeable to us, and to cast a melancholy thought or two after those, with whom, perhaps, we have indulged ourselves in whole nights, of mirth and jollity. With such inclinations in my heart I went to my closet yesterday in the evening, and resolved to be sorrowful; upon which occasion I could not but look with disdain upon myself, that though all the reasons which I had to lament the loss of many of my friends are now as forcible as at the moment of their departure, yet did not my heart swell with the same sorrow which I felt at the time; but I could, without tears, reflect upon many pleasing adventures I have had with some, who have long been blended with common earth. Though it is by the benefit of nature, that length of time thus blots out the violence of afflictions; yet, with tempers too much given to pleasure, it is almost necessary to revive the old places of grief in our memory; and ponder step by step on past life, to lead the mind into that sobriety of thought which poises the heart, and makes it beat with due time, without being quickened with desire, or retarded with despair, from its proper and equal motion. When we wind up a clock that is out of order, to make it go well for the future, we do not immediately set the hand to the present instant, but we make it strike the round of all its hours, before it can recover the regularity of its time. Such, thought I, shall be my method this evening; and since it is that day of the year which I dedicate to the memory of such in another life as I much delighted in when living, an hour to two shall be sacred to sorrow and their memory, while I run over all the melancholy circumstances of this kind which have occurred to me in my whole life.

The first sense of sorrow I ever knew was upon the death of my father, at which time I was not quite five years of age; but was rather amazed at what all the house meant, than possessed with a real understanding why nobody was willing to play with me. I remember I went into the room where his body lay, and my mother sat weeping alone by it. I had my battledore in my hand, and fell a-beating the coffin, and calling Papa; for, I know not how, I had some slight idea that he was locked up there. My mother caught me in her arms, and, transported beyond all patience of the silent grief she was before in, she almost smothered me in her embraces; and told me in a flood of tears, Papa could not hear me, and would play with me no more, for they were going to put him under ground, whence he could never come to us again. She was a very beautiful woman, of a noble spirit, and there was a dignity in her grief amidst all the wildness of her transport, which, methought, struck me with an instinct of sorrow, that, before I was sensible of what it was to grieve, seized my very soul, and has made pity the weakness of my heart ever since. The mind in infancy is, methinks, like the body in embryo; and receives impressions so forcible, that they are as hard to be removed by reason, as any mark with which a child is born is to be taken away by any future application. Hence it is, that good nature in me is no merit; but having been so frequently overwhelmed with her tears before I knew the cause of any affliction, or could draw defences from my own judgement, I imbibed commiseration, remorse, and an unmanly gentleness of mind, which has since ensnared me into ten thousand calamities; and from whence I can reap no advantage, except it be, that, in such a humour as I am now in, I can the better indulge myself in the softnesses of humanity, and enjoy that sweet anxiety which arises from the memory of past afflictions.

We, that are very old, are better able to remember things which befell us in our distant youth, than the passages of later days. For this reason it is, that the companions of my strong and vigorous years present themselves more immediately to me in this office of sorrow. Untimely and unhappy deaths are what we are most apt to lament; so little are we able to make it indifferent when a thing happens, though we know it must happen. Thus we groan under life, and bewail those who are relieved from it. Every object that returned to our imagination raises different passions, according to the circumstance of their departure. Who can have lived in an army, and in a serious hour reflect upon the many gay and agreeable men that might long have flourished in the arts of peace, and not join with the imprecations of the fatherless and widows on the tyrant to whose ambition they fell sacrifices? But gallant men, who are cut off by the sword, move rather our veneration than our pity; and we gather relief enough from their own contempt of death, to make that no evil, which was approached with so much cheerfulness, and attended with so much honour. But when we turn our thoughts from the great parts of life on such occasions, and instead of lamenting those who stood ready to give death to those from whom they had the fortune to receive it; I say, when we let our thoughts wander from such noble objects, and consider the havoc which is made among the tender and the innocent, pity enters with an unmixed softness, and possesses all our souls at once.

Here (were there words to express such sentiments with proper tenderness) I should record the beauty, innocence, and untimely death, of the first object my eyes ever beheld with love. The beauteous virgin! how ignorantly did she charm, how carelessly excel! Oh death! thou hast right to the bold, to the ambitious, to the high, and to the haughty; but why this cruelty to the humble, to the meek, to the undiscerning, to the thoughtless? Nor age, nor business, nor distress, can erase the dear image from my imagination. In the same week I saw her dressed for a ball, and in a shroud. How ill did the habit of death become the pretty trifler! I still behold the smiling earth — A large train of disasters were coming on to my memory, when my servant knocked at my closet-door, and interrupted me with a letter, attended with a hamper of wine, of the same sort with that which is to be put to sale on Thursday next, at Garraway's coffee-house. Upon the receit of it, I sent for three of my friends. We are so intimate, that we can be company in whatever state of mind we meet, and can entertain each other without expecting always to rejoice. The wine we found to be generous and warming, but with such a heat as moved us rather to be cheerful than frolicsome. It revived the spirits, without firing the blood. We commended it until two of the clock this morning; and having to-day met a little before dinner, we found, that though we drank two bottles a man, we had much more reason to recollect than forget what had passed the night before.

On Running After One's Hat

Gilbert K. Chesterton (1874-1936)

The doctor Johnson of the 20th century, he was a fabulous figure in energy and enthusiasm, in paradox and productivity. After entering journalism in 1990, he proceeded to turn out articles, essays, poems, plays, biographies, detective stroieo, and novels with incredible gusto.

I feel an almost savage envy on hearing that London has been flooded in my absence, while I am in the mere country. My own Battersea has been, I understand, particularly favored as a meeting of the waters. Battersea was already, as I need hardly say, the most beautiful of human localities. Now that it has the additional splendor of great sheets of water, there must be something quite incomparable in the landscape (or waterscape) of my romantic town. Battersea must be a vision of Venice. The boat that brought the meat from the butcher's must have shot along those lanes of rippling silver with the strange smoothness of a gondola. The greengrocer who brought cabbages to the corner of the Latchmere Road must have leant upon the oar with the unearthly grace of the gondolier. There is nothing so perfectly poetical as an island; and when a district is flooded it becomes an archipelago.

Some consider such romantic views of flood or fire slightly

lacking in reality. But really this romantic view of such inconveniences is quite as practical as the other. The true optimist who sees in such things an opportunity for enjoyment is quite as logical and much more sensible than the ordinary "indignant Ratepayer" who sees in them an opportunity for grumbling. Real pain, as in the case of being burnt at Smithfield or having a toothache, is a positive thing; it can be supported, but scarcely enjoyed. But, after all, our toothaches are the exception, and as for being burnt at Smithfield, it only happens to us at the very longest intervals. And most of the inconveniences that make men swear or women cry are really sentimental or imaginative inconveniences — things altogether of the mind. For instance, we often hear grown-up people complaining of having to hang about a railway station and wait for a train. Did you ever hear a small boy complain of having to hang about a railway station and wait for a train? No; for to him to be inside a railway station is to be inside a cavern of wonder and a palace of poetical pleasures. Because to him the red light and the green light on the signal are like a new sun and new moon. Because to him when the wooden arm of the signal falls down suddenly, it is as if a great king had thrown down his staff as a signal and started a shrieking tournament of trains. I myself am of little boys' habit in this matter. They also serve who only stand and wait for the two-fifteen. Their meditations may be full of rich and fruitful things. Many of the most purple hours of my life have been passed at Clapham Junction, which is now, I suppose, under water. I have been there in many moods so fixed and mystical that the water might well have come up to my waist before I noticed it particularly. But, in the case of all such annoyances, as I have said, everything depends upon the emotional point of view. You can safely apply the test to almost every one of the things that are currently talked of as the typical nuisances of daily life.

For instance, there is a current impression that it is unpleasant to have to run after one's hat. Why should it be unpleasant to the well-ordered and pious mind? Not merely because it is running, and running exhausts one. The same people run much faster in games and sports. The same people run much more eagerly after an uninteresting little leather ball than they will after a nice silk hat. There is an idea that it is humiliating to run after one's hat, and when people say it is humiliating they mean that it is comic. It certainly is comic; but man is a very comic creature, and most of the things he does are comic — eating, for instance. And the most comic things of all are exactly the things that are most worth doing — such as making love. A man running after a hat is not half so ridiculous as a man running after a wife.

Now a man could, if he felt rightly in the matter, run after his hat with the manliest ardor and the most sacred joy. He might regard himself as a jolly huntsman pursuing a wild animal, for certainly no animal could be wilder. In fact, I am ingood for a man to realise that he is "the heir of all the ages" is pretty commonly admitted; it is a less popular but equally important point that it is good for him sometimes to realise that he is not only an ancestor, but an ancestor of primal antiquity; it is good for him to wonder whether he is not a hero, and to experience ennobling doubts as to whether he is not a solar myth.

The matters which most thoroughly evoke this sense of the abiding childhood of the world are those which are really fresh, abrupt, and inventive in any age; and if we were asked, what was the best proof of this adventurous youth in the nineteenth century we should say, with all respect to its portentous sciences and philosophies, that it was to be found in the rhymes of Mr. Edward Lear and in the literature of nonsense. *The Dong with the Luminous Nose*, at least, is original, as the first ship and the first plough were original.

It is true in a certain sense that some of the greatest writers the world has seen — Aristophanes, Rabelais, and Sterne — have written nonsense; but unless we are mistaken, it is in a widely different sense. The nonsense of these men was satiric — that is to say, symbolic; it was a kind of exuberant capering round a discovered truth. There is all the difference in the world between the instinct of satire, which, seeing in the Kaiser's moustaches something typical of him, draws them continually larger and larger; and the instinct of nonsense which, for no reason whatever, imagines what those moustaches would look like on the present Archbishop of Canterbury if he grew them in a fit of absence of mind. We incline to think that no age except our own could have understood that the Quangle-Wangle meant absolutely nothing, and the Lands of the Jumblies were absolutely nowhere. We fancy that if the account of the knave's trial in *Alice in Wonderland* had been published in the seventeenth century it would have been bracketed with Bunyan's *Trial of Faithful* as a parody on the state prosecutions of the time. We fancy that if *The Dong with the Luminous Nose* had appeared in the same period every one would have called it a dull satire on Oliver Cromwell.

It is altogether advisedly that we quote chiefly from Mr. Lear's *Nonsense Rhymes*. To our mind he is both chronologically and essentially the father of nonsense; we think him superior to Lewis Carroll. In one sense, indeed, Lewis Carroll has a great advantage. We know what Lewis Carroll was in daily life: he was a singularly serious and conventional don, universally respected, but very much of a pedant and something of a Philistine. Thus his strange double life in earth and in dreamland emphasises the idea that lies at the back of nonsense — the idea of *escape*, of escape into a world where things are not fixed horribly in an eternal appropriateness, where apples grow on pear trees, and any odd man you meet may have three legs. Lewis Carroll, living one life in which he would have thundered morally against any one who walked on the wrong plot of grass, and another life in which he would cheerfully call the sun green and the moon blue, was, by his very divided nature, his one foot on both worlds, a perfect type of the position of modern nonsense. His Wonderland is a country populated by insane mathematicians. We feel the whole is an escape into a world of masquerade; we feel that if we could pierce their disguises, we might discover that Humpty Dumpty and the March Hare were Professors and Doctors of Divinity enjoying a mental holiday. This sense of escape is certainly less emphatic in Edward Lear, because of the completeness of his citizenship in the world of unreason. We do not know his prosaic biography as we know Lewis Carroll's. We accept him as a purely fabulous figure, on his own description of himself:

His body is perfectly spherical,
He weareth a runcible hat.

While Lewis Carroll's Wonderland is purely intellectual, Lear introduces quite another element — the element of the poetical and even emotional. Carroll works by the pure reason, but this is not so strong a contrast; for, after all, mankind in the main has always regarded reason as a bit of a joke. Lear introduces his unmeaning words and his amorphous creatures not with the pomp of reason, but with the romantic prelude of rich hues and haunting rhythms,

Far and few, far and few,
Are the lands where the Jumblies live,

is an entirely different type of poetry to that exhibited in *Jabberwocky*. Carroll, with a sense of mathematical neatness, makes his whole poem a mosaic of new and mysterious words. But Edward Lear, with more subtle and placid effrontery, is always introducing scraps of his own elvish dialect into the middle of simple and rational statements, until we are almost stunned into admitting that we know what they mean. There is a genial ring of common sense about such lines as,

> For his aunt Jobiska said "Every one knows
> That a Pobble is better without his toes,"

which is beyond the reach of Carroll. The poet seems so easy on the matter that we are almost driven to pretend that we see his meaning, that we know the peculiar difficulties of a Pobble, that we are as old travellers in the "Gromboolian Plain" as he is.

Our claim that nonsense is a new literature (we might almost say a new sense) would be quite indefensible if nonsense were nothing more than a mere aesthetic fancy. Nothing sublimely artistic has ever arisen out of mere art, any more than anything essentially reasonable has ever arisen out of the pure reason. There must always be a rich moral soil for any great aesthetic growth. The principle of *art for art's sake* is a very good principle if it means that there is a vital distinction between the earth and the tree that has its roots in the earth; but it is a very bad principle if it means that the tree could grow just as well with its roots in the air. Every great literature has always been allegorical — allegorical of some view of the whole universe. The *Iliad* is only great because all life is a battle, the *Odyssey* because all life is a journey, the Book of Job because all life is a riddle. There is one attitude in which we think that all existence is summed up in the word "ghosts"; another, and somewhat better one, in which we think it is summed up in the words *A Midsummer Night's Dream*. Even the vulgarest melodrama or detective story can be good if it expresses something of the delight in sinister possibilities — the healthy lust for darkness and terror which may come on us any night in walking down a dark lane. If, therefore, nonsense is really to be the literature of the future, it must have its own version of the Cosmos to offer; the world must not only be tragic, romantic, and religious, it must be nonsensical also. And here we fancy that nonsense will, in a very unexpected way, come to the aid of the spiritual view of things. Religion has for centuries been trying to make men exult in the "wonders" of creation, but it has forgotten that a thing cannot be completely wonderful so long as it remains sensible. So long as we regard a tree as an obvious thing, naturally and reasonably created for a giraffe to eat, we cannot properly wonder at it. It is when we consider it as a prodigious wave of the living soil sprawling up to the skies for no reason in particular that we take off our hats, to the astonishment of the park-keeper. Everything has in fact another side to it, like the moon, the patroness of nonsense. Viewed from that other side, a bird is a blossom broken loose from its chain of stalk, a man a quadruped begging on its hind legs, a house a gigantesque hat to cover a man from the sun, a chair an apparatus of four wooden legs for a cripple with only two.

This is the side of things which tends most truly to spiritual wonder. It is significant that in the greatest religious poem existent, the Book of Job, the argument which convinces the infidel is not (as has been represented by the merely rational religionism of the eighteenth century) a picture of the ordered beneficence of the Creation; but, on the contrary, a picture of the huge and undecipherable unreason of it. "Hast Thou sent the rain upon the desert where no man is?" This simple sense of wonder at the shapes of things, and at their exuberant independence of our intellectual standards and our trivial definitions, is the basis of spirituality as it is the basis of nonsense. Nonsense and faith (strange as the conjunction may seem) are the two supreme symbolic assertions of the truth that to draw out the soul of things with a syllogism is as impossible as to draw out Leviathan with a hook. The well-meaning person who, by merely studying the logical side of things, has decided that "faith is nonsense" does not know how truly he speaks; later it may come back to him in the form that nonsense is faith.

On the Knocking at the Gate in Macbeth

Thomas de Quincey (1785-1859)

English essayist and critic. De Quincey is famous for *Confessions of an English Opium Eater*, a fascinating memoir distinguished by great imaginative power and prose that is splendid and elaborate without stiffness. These qualities are also present in his personal and fugitive essays such as *Suspiria de Profundis* (1845) and *The English Mail Coach* (1849). One of the major critics of the romantic movement, he had clear, judicious taste and remarkable insight, and was learned and original though sometimes prolix and vague. He was closely associated with Wordsworth and Coleridge, residing for a time in the Lake Country, and was also acquainted with Lamb, Hazlitt, Hood, and other literary figures.

From my boyish days I had always felt a great perplexity on one point in *Macbeth*. It was this: the knocking at the gate, which succeeds to the murder of Duncan, produced to my feelings an effect for which I never could account. The effect was, that it reflected back upon the murderer a peculiar awfulness and a depth of solemnity; yet, however obstinately I endeavoured with my understanding to comprehend this, for many years I never could see *why* it should produce such an effect.

Here I pause for one moment, to exhort the reader never to pay any attention to his understanding, when it stands in opposition to any other faculty of his mind. The mere understanding, however useful and indispensable, is the meanest faculty in the human mind, and the most to be distrusted; and yet the great majority of people trust to nothing else, which may do for ordinary life, but not for philosophical purposes. Of this out of ten thousand instances that I might produce, I will cite one. Ask of any person whatsoever, who is not previously prepared for the demand by a knowledge of the perspective, to draw in the rudest way the commonest appearance which depends upon the laws of that science; as, for instance, to represent the effect of two walls standing at right angles to each other, or the appearance of the houses on each side of a street, as seen by a person looking down the street from one extremity. Now in all cases, unless the person has happened to observe in pictures how it is that artists produce these effects, he will be utterly unable to make the smallest approximation to it. Yet why? For he has actually seen the effect every day of his life. The reason is — that he allows his understanding to overrule his eyes. His understanding, which includes no intuitive knowledge of the laws of vision, can furnish him with no reason why a line which is known and can be proved to be a horizontal line, should not appear a horizontal line; a line that made any angle with the perpendicular, less than a right angle, would seem to him to indicate that his houses were all tumbling down together. Accordingly, he makes the line of his houses a horizontal line, and fails, of course, to produce the effect demanded. Here, then, is one instance out of many, in which not only the understanding is allowed to overrule the eyes, but where the understanding is positively allowed to obliterate the eyes, as it were; for not only does the man believe the evidence of his understanding in opposition to that of his eyes, but (what is monstrous!) the idiot is not aware that his eyes ever gave such evidence. He does not know that he has seen (and therefore *quoad* his consciousness has *not* seen) that which *has* seen every day of his life.

But to return from this digression, my understanding could furnish no reason why the knocking at the gate in *Macbeth* should produce any effect, direct or reflected. In fact, my understanding said positively that it could *not* produce any effect. But I knew better; I felt that it did; and I waited and clung to the problem until further knowledge should enable me to solve it. At length, in 1812, Mr. Williams made his *début* on the stage of Ratcliffe Highway, and executed those unparalleled murders which have procured for him such a brilliant and undying reputation. On which murders, by the way, I must observe, that in one respect they have had an ill effect, by making the connoisseur in murder very fastidious in his taste, and dissatisfied by anything that has been since done in that line. All other murders look pale by the deep crimson of his; and, as an amateur once said to me in a querulous tone, "There has been absolutely nothing *doing* since his time, or nothing that's worth speaking of." But this is wrong; for it is unreasonable to expect all men to be great artists, and born with the genius of Mr. Williams. Now it will be remembered, that in the first of these murders (that of the Marrs), the same incident (of a knocking at the door, soon after the work of extermination was complete) did actually occur, which the genius of Shakespeare has invented; and all good judges, and the most eminent dilettanti, acknowledged the felicity of Shakespeare's suggestion, as soon as it was actually realized. Here, then, was a fresh proof that I was right in relying on my own feeling, in opposition to my understanding; and I again set myself to study the problem; at length I solved it to my own satisfaction, and my solution is this. Murder, in ordinary cases, where the sympathy is wholly directed to the case of the murdered person, is an incident of coarse and vulgar horror; and for this reason, that it flings the interest exclusively upon the natural but ignoble instinct by which we cleave to life; an instinct which, as being indispensable to the primal law of self-preservation, is the same in kind (though different in degree) amongst all living creatures: this instinct, therefore, because it annihilates all distinctions, and degrades the greatest of men to the level of "the poor beetle that we tread on," exhibits human nature in its most abject and humiliating attitude. Such an attitude would little suit the purposes of the poet. What then must he do? He must throw the interest on the murderer. Our sympathy must be with *him* (of course I mean a sympathy of comprehension, a sympathy by which we enter into his feelings, and are made to understand them, — not a sympathy of pity or approbation). In the murdered person, all strife of thought, all flux and reflux of passion and of purpose, are crushed by one overwhelming panic; the fear of instant death smites him "with its petrific mace." But in the murderer, such a murderer as a poet will condescend to, there must be raging some great storm of passion — jealousy, ambition, vengeance, hatred — which will create a hell within him; and into this hell we are to look.

In *Macbeth*, for the sake of gratifying his own enormous and teeming faculty of creation, Shakespeare has introduced two murderers: and, as usual in his hands, they are remarkably discriminated: but, though in Macbeth the strife of mind is greater than in his wife, the tiger spirit not so awake, and his feelings caught chiefly by contagion from her, — yet, as both were finally involved in the guilt of murder, the murderous mind of necessity is finally to be presumed in both. This was to be expressed; and on its own account, as well as to make it a more proportionable antagonist to the unoffending nature of their victim, "the gracious Duncan," and adequately to expound "the deep damnation of his taking off," this was to be expressed with peculiar energy. We were to be made to feel that the human nature, i.e., the divine nature of love and mercy, spread through the hearts of all creatures, and seldom utterly withdrawn from man — was gone, vanished, extinct; and that the fiendish nature had taken its place. And, as this effect is marvellously accomplished in the *dialogues* and *soliloquies* themselves, so it is finally consummated by the expedient under consideration; and it is to this that I now solicit the reader's attention. If the reader has ever witnessed a wife, daughter, or sister in a fainting-fit, he may chance to have observed that the most affecting moment in such a spectacle is *that* in which a sigh and a stirring announce the recommencement of suspended life. Or, if the reader has ever been present in a vast metropolis, on the day when some great national idol was carried in funeral pomp to his grave, and chancing to walk near the course through which it passed, has felt powerfully in the silence and desertion of the streets, and in the stagnation of ordinary business, the deep interest which at that moment was possessing the heart of man — if all at once he should hear the death-like stillness broken up by the sound of wheels rattling away from the scene, and making known that the transitory vision was dissolved, he will be aware that at no moment was his sense of the complete suspension and pause in ordinary human concerns so full and affecting, as at that moment when the suspension ceases, and the goings-on of human life are suddenly resumed. All action in any direction is best expounded, measured, and made apprehensible, by reaction. Now apply this to the case of *Macbeth*. Here, as I have said, the retiring of the human heart, and the entrance of the fiendish heart was to be expressed and made sensible. Another world has stepped in; and the murderers are taken out of the region of human things, human purposes, human desires. They are transfigured: Lady Macbeth is "unsexed"; Macbeth has forgot that he was born of woman; both are conformed to the image of devils; and the world of devils is suddenly revealed. But how shall this be conveyed and made palpable? In order that a new world may step in, this world must for a time disappear. The murderers, and the murder must be insulated — cut off by an immeasurable gulf from the ordinary tide and succession of human affairs — locked up and sequestered in some deep recess; we must be made sensible that the world of ordinary life is suddenly arrested — laid asleep — tranced — racked into a dread armistice; time must be annihilated; relation to things without abolished; and all must pass self-withdrawn into a deep syncope and suspension of earthly passion. Hence it is, that when the deed is done, when the work of darkness is perfect, then the world of darkness passes away like a pageantry in the clouds: the knocking at the gate is heard; and it makes known audibly that the reaction has commenced; the human has made its reflux upon the fiendish; the pulses of life are beginning to beat again; and the re-establishment of the goings-on of the world in which we live, first makes us profoundly sensible of the awful parenthesis that has suspended them.

O mighty poet! Thy works are not as those of other men, simply and merely great works of art; but are also like the phenomena of nature, like the sun and the sea, the stars and the flowers; like frost and snow, rain and dew, hailstorm and thunder, which are to be studied with entire submission of our own faculties, and in the perfect faith that in them there can be no too much or too little, nothing useless or inert — but that, the further we press in our discoveries, the more we shall see proofs of design and self-supporting arrangement where the careless eye had seen nothing but accident!

HOW SHOULD ONE READ A BOOK?

Virginia Woolf (1882-1941)

English novelist, critic, and essayist, the wife of Leonard Woolf. An exact contemporary of James Joyce, Woolf too is known as an experimenter and innovator in novel writing, particularly in her use of the techniques of interior monologue and stream of consciousness. Her novels are noted for their poetic and symbolic quality; emphasis is not on plot or action but on the psychological realm occupied by her characters. The books are also known for their delicacy and sensitivity of style, their evocation of place and mood, and their background of historical and literary reference.

In the first place, I want to emphasise the note of interrogation at the end of my title. Even if I could answer the question for myself, the answer would apply only to me and not to you. The only advice, indeed, that one person can give another about reading is to take no advice, to follow your own instincts, to use your own reason, to come to your own conclusions. If this is agreed between us, then I feel at liberty to put forward a few ideas and suggestions because you will not allow them to fetter that independence which is the most important quality that a reader can possess. After all, what laws can be laid down about books? The battle of Waterloo was certainly fought on a certain day; but is *Hamlet* a better play than *Lear*? Nobody can say. Each must decide that question for himself. To admit authorities, however heavily furred and gowned, into our libraries and let them tell us how to read, what to read, what value to place upon what we read, is to destroy the spirit of freedom which is the breath of those sanctuaries. Everywhere else we may be bound by laws and conventions — there we have none.

But to enjoy freedom, if the platitude is pardonable, we have of course to control ourselves. We must not squander our powers, helplessly and ignorantly, squirting half the house in order to water a single rose-bush; we must train them, exactly and powerfully, here on the very spot. This, it may be, is one of the first difficulties that faces us in a library. What is "the very spot"? There may well seem to be nothing but a conglomeration and huddle of confusion: Poems and novels, histories and memoirs, dictionaries and blue-books; books written in all languages by men and women of all tempers, races, and ages jostle each other on the shelf. And outside the donkey brays, the women gossip at the pump, the colts gallop across the fields. Where are we to begin? How are we to bring order into this multitudinous chaos and get the deepest and widest pleasure from what we read?

It is simple enough to say that since books have classes — fiction, biography, poetry — we should separate them and take from each what it is right that each should give us. Yet few people ask from books what books can give us. Most commonly we come to books with blurred and divided minds, asking of fiction that it shall be true, of poetry that it shall be false, of biography that it shall be flattering, of history that it shall enforce our own prejudices. If we could banish all such preconceptions when we read, that would be an admirable beginning. Do not dictate to your author; try to become him. Be his fellow-worker and accomplice. If you hang back, and reserve and criticise at first, you are preventing yourself from getting the fullest possible value from what you read. But if you open your mind as widely as possible, then signs and hints of almost imperceptible fineness, from the twist and turn of the first sentences, will bring you into the presence of a human being unlike any other. Steep yourself in this, acquaint yourself with this, and soon you will find that your author is giving you, or attempting to give you, something far more definite. The thirty-two chapters of a novel — if we consider how to read a novel first — are an attempt to make something as formed and controlled as a building: but words are more impalpable than bricks; reading is a longer and more complicated process than seeing. Perhaps the quickest way to understand the elements of what a novelist is doing is not to read, but to write; to make your own experiment with the dangers and difficulties of words. Recall, then, some event that has left a distinct impression on you — how at the corner of the street, perhaps, you passed two people talking. A tree shook; an electric light danced; the tone of the talk was comic, but also tragic; a whole vision, an entire conception, seemed contained in that moment.

But when you attempt to reconstruct it in words, you will find that it breaks into a thousand conflicting impressions. Some must be subdued; others emphasised; in the process you will lose, probably, all grasp upon the emotion itself. Then turn from your blurred and littered pages to the opening pages of some great novelist — Defoe, Jane Austen, Hardy. Now you will be better able to appreciate their mastery. It is not merely that we are in the presence of a different person — Defoe, Jane Austen, or Thomas Hardy — but that we are living in a different world. Here, in *Robinson Crusoe*, we are trudging a plain high road; one thing happens after another; the fact and the order of the fact is enough. But if the open air and adventure mean everything to Defoe they mean nothing to Jane Austen. Hers is the drawing-room, and people talking, and by the many mirrors of their talk revealing their characters. And if, when we have accustomed ourselves to the drawing-room and its reflections, we turn to Hardy, we are once more spun around. The moors are round us and the stars are above our heads. The other side of the mind is now exposed — the dark side that comes uppermost in solitude, not the light side that shows in company. Our relations are not towards people, but towards Nature and destiny. Yet different as these worlds are, each is consistent with itself. The maker of each is careful to observe the laws of his own perspective, and however great a strain they may put upon us they will never confuse us, as lesser writers so frequently do, by introducing two different kinds of reality into the same book. Thus to go from one great novelist to another — from Jane Austen to Hardy, from Peacock to Trollope, from Scott to Meredith — is to be wrenched and uprooted; to be thrown this way and then that. To read a novel is a difficult and complex art. You must be capable not only of great finesse of perception, but of great boldness of imagination if you are going to make use of all that the novelist — the great artist — gives you.

But a glance at the heterogeneous company on the shelf will show you that writers are very seldom "great artists"; far more often a book makes no claim to be a work of art at all. These biographies and autobiographies, for example, lives of great men, of men long dead and forgotten, that stand cheek by jowl with the novels and poems, are we to refuse to read them because they are not "art"? Or shall we read them, but read them in a different way, with a different aim? Shall we read them in the first place to satisfy that curiosity which possesses us sometimes when in the evening we linger in front of a house where the lights are lit and the blinds not yet drawn, and each floor of the house shows us a different section of human life in being? Then we are consumed with curiosity about the lives of these people — the servants gossiping, the gentlemen dining, the girl dressing for a party, the old woman at the window with her knitting. Who are they, what are they, what are their names, their occupations, their thoughts, and adventures?

Biographies and memoirs answer such questions, light up innumerable such houses; they show us people going about their daily affairs, toiling, failing, succeeding, eating, hating, loving, until they die. And sometimes as we watch, the house fades and the iron railings vanish and we are out at sea; we are hunting, sailing, fighting; we are among savages and soldiers; we are taking part in great campaigns. Or if we like to stay here in England, in London, still the scene changes; the street narrows; the house becomes small, cramped, diamond-paned, and malodorous. We see a poet, Donne, driven from such a house because the walls were so thin that when the children cried their voices cut through them. We can follow him, through the paths that lie in the pages of books, to Twickenham; to Lady Bedford's Park, a famous meeting-ground for nobles and poets; and then turn our steps to Wilton, the great house under the downs, and hear Sidney read the *Arcadia* to his sister; and ramble among the very marshes and see the very herons that figure in that famous romance; and then again travel north with that other Lady Pembroke, Anne Clifford, to her wild moors, or plunge into the city and control our merriment at the sight of Gabriel Harvey in his black velvet suit arguing about poetry with Spenser. Nothing is more fascinating than to grope and stumble in the alternate darkness and splendour of Elizabethan London. But there is no staying there. The Temples and the Swifts, the Harleys and the St. Johns beckon us on; hour upon hour can be spent disentangling their quarrels and deciphering their characters; and when we tire of them we can stroll on, past a lady in black wearing diamonds, to Samuel Johnson and Goldsmith and Garrick; or cross the channel, if we like, and meet Voltaire and Diderot, Madame du Deffand; and so back to England and Twickenham — how certain places repeat themselves and certain names! — where Lady Bedford had her Park once and Pope lived later, to Walpole's home at Strawberry Hill. But Walpole introduces us to such a swarm of new acquaintances, there are so many houses to visit and bells to ring that we may well hesitate for a moment, on the Miss Berrys' doorstep, for example, when behold, up comes Thackeray; he is the friend of the woman whom Walpole loved; so that merely by going from friend to friend, from garden to garden, from house to house, we have passed from one end of English literature to another and wake to find ourselves here again in the present, if we can so differentiate this moment from all that have gone before. This, then, is one of the ways in which we can read these lives and letters; we can make them light up the many windows of the past; we can watch the famous dead in their familiar habits and fancy sometimes that we are very close and can surprise their secrets, and sometimes we may pull out a play or a poem that they have written and see whether it reads differently in the presence of the author. But this again rouses other questions. How far, we must ask ourselves, is a book influenced by its writer's life — how far is it safe to let the man interpret the writer? How far shall we resist or give way to the sympathies and antipathies that the man himself rouses in us — so sensitive are words, so receptive of the character of the author? These are questions that press upon us when we read lives and letters, and we must answer them for ourselves, for nothing can be more fatal than to be guided by the preferences of others in a matter so personal.

But also we can read such books with another aim, not to throw light on literature, not to become familiar with famous people, but to refresh and exercise our own creative powers. Is there not an open window on the right hand of the bookcase? How delightful to stop reading and look out! How stimulating the scene is, in its unconsciousness, its irrelevance, its perpetual movement — the colts galloping round the field, the woman filling her pail at the well, the donkey throwing back his head and emitting his long, acrid moan. The greater part of any library is nothing but the record of such fleeting moments in the lives of men, women, and donkeys. Every literature, as it grows old, has its rubbish-heap, its records of vanished moments and forgotten lives told in faltering and feeble accents that have perished. But if you give yourself up to the delight of rubbish-reading you will be surprised, indeed you will be overcome, by the relics of human life that have been cast out to moulder. It may be one letter — but what a vision it gives! It may be a few sentences — but what vistas they suggest! Sometimes a whole story will come together with such beautiful humour and pathos and completeness that it seems as if a great novelist had been at work, yet it is only an old actor, Tate Wilkinson, remembering the strange story of Captain Jones; it is only a young subaltern serving under Arthur Wellesley and falling in love with a pretty girl at Lisbon; it is only Maria Allen letting fall her sewing in the empty drawing-room and sighing how she wishes she had taken Dr. Burney's good advice and had never eloped with her Rishy. None of this has any value; it is negligible in the extreme; yet how absorbing it is now and again to go through the rubbish-heaps and find rings and scissors and broken noses buried in the huge past and try to piece them together while the colt gallops round the field, the woman fills her pail at the well, and the donkey brays.

But we tire of rubbish-reading in the long run. We tire of searching for what is needed to complete the half-truth which is all that the Wilkinsons, the Bunburys, and the Maria Allens are able to offer us. They had not the artist's power of mastering and eliminating; they could not tell the whole truth even about their own lives; they have disfigured the story that might have been so shapely. Facts are all that they can offer us, and facts are a very inferior form of fiction. Thus the desire grows upon us to have done with half-statements and approximations; to cease from searching out the minute shades of human character, to enjoy the greater abstractness, the purer truth of fiction. Thus we create the mood, intense and generalised, unaware of detail, but stressed by some regular, recurrent beat, whose natural expression is poetry; and that is the time to read poetry when we are almost able to write it.

> Western wind, when wilt thou blow?
> The small rain down can rain.
> Christ, if my love were in my arms,
> And I in my bed again!

The impact of poetry is so hard and direct that for the moment there is no other sensation except that of the poem itself. What profound depths we visit then — how sudden and complete is our immersion! There is nothing here to catch hold of; nothing to stay us in our flight. The illusion of fiction is gradual; its effects are prepared; but who when they read these four lines stops to ask who wrote them, or conjures up the thought of Donne's house or Sidney's secretary; or enmeshes them in the intricacy of the past and the succession of generations? The poet is always our contemporary. Our being for the moment is centred and constricted, as in any violent shock of personal emotion. Afterwards, it is true, the sensation begins to spread in wider rings through our minds; remoter senses are reached; these begin to sound and to comment and we are aware of echoes and reflections. The intensity of poetry covers an immense range of emotion. We have only to compare the force and directness of

> I shall fall like a tree, and find my grave
> Only remembering that I grieve,

with the wavering modulation of

> Minutes are numbered by the fall of sands,
> As by an hour glass; the span of time
> Doth waste us to our graves, and we look on it;
> An age of pleasure, revelled out, comes home
> At last and ends in sorrow; but the life,
> Weary of riot, numbers every sand,
> Wailing in sighs, until the last drop down,
> So to conclude calamity in rest,

or place the meditative calm of

> whether we be young or old,
> Our destiny, our being's heart and home,

> Is with infinitude, and only there;
> With hope it is, hope that can never die,
> Effort, and expectation, and desire,
> And something evermore about to be,

besides the complete and inexhaustible loveliness of

> The moving Moon went up the sky,
> And no where did abide:
> Softly she was going up,
> And a star or two beside —

or the splendid fantasy of

> And the woodland haunter
> Shall not cease to saunter
> When, far down some glade,
> Of the great world's burning,
> One soft flame upturning
> Seems, to his discerning,
> Crocus in the shade.

to bethink us of the varied art of the poet; his power to make us at once actors and spectators; his power to run his hand into character as if it were a glove, and be Falstaff or Lear; his power to condense, to widen, to state, once and for ever. "We have only to compare" — with those words the cat is out of the bag, and the true complexity of reading is admitted. The first process, to receive impressions with the utmost understanding, is only half the process of reading; it must be completed, if we are to get the whole pleasure from a book, by another. We must pass judgement upon these multitudinous impressions; we must make of these fleeting shapes one that is hard and lasting. But not directly. Wait for the dust of reading to settle; for the conflict and the questioning to die down; walk, talk, pull the dead petals from a rose, or fall asleep. Then suddenly without our willing it, for it is thus that Nature undertakes these transitions, the book will return, but differently. It will float to the top of the mind as a whole. And the book as a whole is different from the book received currently in separate phrases. Details now fit themselves into their places. We see the shape from start to finish; it is a barn, a pig-sty, or a cathedral. Now then we can compare book with book as we compare building with building. But this act of comparison means that our attitude has changed; we are no longer the friends of the writer, but his judges; and just as we cannot be too sympathetic as friends, so as judges we cannot be too severe. Are they not criminals, books, that have wasted our time and sympathy; are they not the most insidious enemies of society, corrupters, defilers, the writers of false books, faked books, books that fill the air with decay and disease? Let us then be severe in our judgements; let us compare each book with the greatest of its kind. There they hang in the mind the shapes of the books we have read solidified by the judgements we have passed on them — *Robinson Crusoe*, *Emma*, *The Return of the Native*. Compare the novels with these — even the latest and least of novels has a right to be judged with the best. And so with poetry — when the intoxication of rhythm has died down and the splendour of words has faded a visionary shape will return to us and this must be compared with *Lear*, with *Phédre*, with *The Prelude*, or if not with these, with whatever is the best or seem to us to be the best in its own kind. And we may be sure that the newness of new poetry and fiction is its most superficial quality and that we have only to alter slightly, not to recast, the standards by which we have judged the old.

It would be foolish, then, to pretend that the second part of reading, to judge, to compare, is as simple as the first — to open the mind wide to the fast flocking of innumerable impressions. To continue reading without the book before you, to hold one shadow-shape against another, to have read widely enough and with enough understanding to make such comparisons alive and illuminating — that is difficult; it is still more difficult to press further and to say, "Not only is the book of this sort, but it is of this value; here it fails; here it succeeds; this is bad, that is good." To carry out this part of a reader's duty needs such imagination, insight, and learning that it is hard to conceive any one mind sufficiently endowed, impossible for the most self-confident to find more than the seeds of such powers in himself. Would it not be wiser, then, to remit this part of reading and to allow the critics, the gowned and furred authorities of the library, to decide the question of the book's absolute value for us? Yet how impossible! We may stress the value of sympathy; we may try to sink our own identity as we read. But we know that we cannot sympathise wholly or immerse ourselves wholly; there is always a demon in us who whispers, "I hate, I love," and we cannot silence him. Indeed, it is precisely because we hate and we love that our relation with the poets and novelists is so intimate that we find the presence of another person intolerable. And even if the results are abhorrent and our judgments are wrong, still our taste, the nerve of sensation that sends shocks through us, is our chief illuminant; we learn through feeling; we cannot suppress our own idiosyncrasy without impoverishing it. But as time goes on perhaps we can train our taste; perhaps we can make it submit to some control. When it has fed greedily and lavishly upon books of all sorts — poetry, fiction, history, biography — and has stopped reading and looked for long spaces upon the variety, the incongruity of the living world, we shall find that it is changing a little; it is not so greedy, it is more reflective. It will begin to bring us not merely judgments on particular books, but it will tell us that there is a quality common to certain books. Listen, it will say, what shall we call *this*? And it will read us perhaps *Lear* and then perhaps *Agamemnon* in order to bring out that common quality. Thus, with our taste to guide us, we shall venture beyond the particular book in search of qualities that group books together; we shall give them names and thus frame a rule that brings order into our perceptions. We shall gain a further and a rarer pleasure from that discrimination. But as a rule only lives when it is perpetually broken by contact with the books themselves — nothing is easier and more stultifying than to make rules which exist out of touch with facts, in a vacuum — now at least, in order to steady ourselves in this difficult attempt, it may be well to turn to the very rare writers who are able to enlighten us upon literature as an art. Coleridge and Dryden and Johnson, in their considered criticism, the poets and novelists themselves in their unconsidered sayings, are often surprisingly relevant; they light up and solidify the vague ideas that have been tumbling in the misty depths of out minds. But they are only able to help us if we come to them laden with questions and suggestions won honestly in the course of our own reading. They can do nothing for us if we herd ourselves under their authority and lie down like sheep in the shade of a hedge. We can only understand their ruling when it comes in conflict with our own and vanquishes it.

If this is so, if to read a book as it should be read calls for the rarest qualities of imagination, insight, and judgment, you may perhaps, conclude that literature is a very complex art and that it is unlikely that we shall be able, even after a lifetime of reading, to make any valuable contribution to its criticism. We must remain readers; we shall not put on the further glory that belongs to those rare beings who are also critics. But still we have our responsibilities as readers and even our importance. The standards we raise and the judgments we pass steal into the air and become part of the atmosphere which writers breathe as they work. An influence is created which tells upon them even if it never finds its way into print. And that influence, if it were well instructed, vigorous and individual and sincere, might be of great value now when criticism is necessarily in abeyance; when books pass in review like the procession of animals in a shooting gallery, and the critic has only one second in which to load and aim and shoot and may well be pardoned if he mistakes rabbits for tigers, eagles for barn-door fowls, or misses altogether and wastes his shot upon some peaceful sow grazing in a further field. If behind the erratic gunfire of the press the author felt that there was another kind of criticism, the opinion of people reading for the love of reading, slowly and unprofessionally, and judging with great sympathy and yet with great severity, might this not improve the quality of his work? And if by our means books were to become stronger, richer, and more varied, that would be an end worth reaching.

Yet who reads to bring about an end however desirable? Are there not some pursuits that we practise because they are good in themselves, and some pleasures that are final? And is not this among them? I have sometimes dreamt, at least, that when the Day of Judgment dawns and the great conquerors and lawyers and statesmen come to receive their rewards — their crowns, their laurels, their names carved indelibly upon imperishable marble — the Almighty will turn to Peter and will say, not without a certain envy when He sees us coming with our books under our arms, "Look, these need no reward. We have nothing to give them here. They have loved reading."

Section II : Culture

REPORT FROM EL DORADO

Michael Ventura

Michael Ventura writes a column on popular culture and ideas for the L.A. Weekly. Some of these articles are collected in the 1985 book *Shadow Dancing in the U.S.A.* For many Americans, watching television is simply a way to block out the daily stress of work or school or personal problems. It might seem, then, that analyzing such a medium is to give it too much credit. It is, in fact, easy to dismiss most television programming as mere entertainment, but Ventura argues in the following article that we must pay attention to this medium, because "It *means* something to watch so much TV."

To go from a job you don't like to watching a screen on which others live more intensely than you ... is American life, by and large. This is our political ground. This is our artistic ground. This is what we've done with our immense resources. We have to stop calling it "entertainment" or "news" or "sports" and start calling it what it is: our most immediate environment.

This is a very, very different America from the America that built the industrial capacity to win the Second World War and to surge forward on the multiple momentums of that victory for thirty years. That was an America that worked at mostly menial tasks during the day (now we work at mostly clerical tasks) and had to look at each other at night.

I'm not suggesting a nostalgia for that time. It was repressive and bigoted to an extent that is largely forgotten today, to cite only two of its uglier aspects. But in that environment America meant *America*: the people and the land. The land was far bigger than what we'd done with the land.

This is no longer true. Now the environment of America is media. Not the land itself, but the image of the land. The focus is not on the people so much as it is on the interplay between people and screens. What we've done with the land is far more important now than the land — we're not even dealing with the land anymore, we're dealing with our manipulation and pollution of it.

And what we've done with the very concept of "image" is taking on far more importance for many of us than the actual sights and sounds of our lives.

For instance: Ronald Reagan stands on a cliff in Normandy to commemorate the day U.S. Army Rangers scaled those cliffs in the World War II invasion. Today's Rangers reenact the event while some of the original Rangers, in their sixties now, look on. Except that it is the wrong cliff. The cliff that was actually scaled is a bit further down the beach, but it's not as photogenic as this cliff, so this cliff has been chosen for everybody to emote over. Some of the old Rangers tell reporters that the historical cliff is over yonder, but the old Rangers are swept up (as well they might be) in the ceremonies, and nobody objects enough. This dislocation, this choice, this stance that the real cliff is not important, today's photograph is more important, is a media event. It insults the real event, and overpowers it. Multiplied thousands of times over thousands of outlets of every form and size, ensconced in textbooks as well as screenplays, in sales presentations as well as legislative packages, in religious revivals as well as performance-art pieces, this is the process that has displaced what used to be called "culture."

"I'm not even sure it's a culture anymore. It's like this careening hunger splattering out in all directions."

Jeff Nightbyrd was trying to define "culture" in the wee hours at the Four Queens in Las Vegas. It was a conversation that had been going on since we'd become friends working on the *Austin Sun* in 1974, trying to get our bearings now that the sixties were *really over*. He'd spent that tripletime decade as an SDS organizer and editor of *Rat*, and I'd hit Austin after a few years of road-roving, commune-hopping, and intensive (often depressive) self-exploration — getting by, as the song said, with a little help from my friends, as a lot of us did then. This particular weekend Nightbyrd had come to Vegas from Austin for a computer convention, and I had taken off from my duties at the *L.A. Weekly* for some lessons in craps (at which Jeff is quite good) and to further our rap. The slot machines clattered around us in unison, almost comfortingly, the way the sound of a large shaky air-conditioner can be comforting in a cheap hotel room when you're trying to remember to forget. We were, after all, trying to fathom an old love: America.

There are worse places to indulge in this obsession than Las

Vegas. It is the most American, the most audacious, of cities. Consuming unthinkable amounts of energy in the midst of an unlivable desert (Death Valley is not far away), its decor is based on various cheap-to-luxurious versions of a 1930s Busby Berkeley musical. Indeed, no studio backlot could ever be more of a set, teeming with extras, people who come from all over America, and all over the world, to see the topless, tasteless shows, the Johnny Carson guests on parade doing their utterly predictable routines, the dealers and crap-table croupiers who combine total boredom with ruthless efficiency and milk us dry — yet at least these tourists are risking something they genuinely value: money. It's a quiz show turned into a way of life, where you can get a good Italian dinner at dawn. Even the half-lit hour of the wolf doesn't faze Las Vegas. How could it, when the town has survived the flash of atom bombs tested just over the horizon?

The history books will tell you that, ironically enough, the town was founded by Mormons in 1855. Even their purity of vision couldn't bear the intensity of this desert, and they abandoned the place after just two years. But they had left a human imprint, and a decade later the U.S. Army built a fort here. The settlement hung on, and the railroad came through in 1905. During the Second World War the Mafia started to build the city as we know it now. Religious zealots, the Army, and the Mafia — quite a triad of founding fathers.

Yet one could go back even further, some 400 years, when the first Europeans discovered the deserts of the American West —

Spaniards who, as they slowly began to believe that there might be no end to these expansive wilds, became more and more certain that somewhere, somewhere to the north, lay El Dorado — a city of gold. Immeasurable wealth would be theirs, they believed, and eternal youth. What would they have thought if they had suddenly come upon modern Las Vegas, lying as it does in the midst of this bleached nowhere, glowing at night with a brilliance that would have frightened them? We have built our desert city to their measure — for they were gaudy and greedy, devout and vicious, jovial and frenzied, like this town. They had just wasted the entire Aztec civilization because their fantasies were so strong they couldn't see the ancient cultural marvels before their eyes. The Aztecs, awed and terrified, believed they were being murdered by gods; and in the midst of such strangeness, the Spaniards took on godlike powers even in their own eyes. As many Europeans would in America, they took liberties here they would never have taken within sight of their home cathedrals. Their hungers dominated them, and in their own eyes the New World seemed as inexhaustible as their appetites. So when Nightbyrd described our present culture as "a careening hunger splattering out in all directions," he was also, if unintentionally, speaking about our past. Fittingly, we were sitting in the midst of a city that had been fantasized by those seekers of El Dorado 400 years ago. In that sense, America had Las Vegas a century before it had Plymouth Rock. And our sensibility has been caught between the fantasies of the conquistadors and the obsessions of the Puritans ever since.

Yes, a fitting place to try to think about American culture.

"There are memories of culture," Nightbyrd was saying, "but the things that have given people strength have dissolved. And because they're dissolved, people are into distractions. And distractions aren't culture."

Are there even memories? The media have taken over our memories. That day Nightbyrd had been driving through the small towns that dot this desert, towns for which Vegas is only a dull glow to the southwest. In a bar in one of those towns, "like that little bar in *The Right Stuff*," he'd seen pictures of cowboys on the wall. "Except that they weren't cowboys. They were movie stars. Guys who grew up in Glendale [John Wayne] and Santa Monica [Robert Redford]." Surely this desert had its own heroes once, in the old gold-mining towns where a few people still hang on, towns like Goldfield and Tonopah. Remembering those actual heroes would be "culture." Needing pictures of movie stars for want of the real thing is only a nostalgia for culture.

Nostalgia is not memory. Memory is specific. One has a relationship to a memory, and it may be a difficult relationship, because a memory always makes a demand upon the present. But nostalgia is vague, a sentimental wash that obscures memory and acts as a narcotic to dull the importance of the present.

Media as we know it now thrives on nostalgia and is hostile to memory. In a television bio-pic, Helen Keller is impersonated by Mare Winningham. But the face of Helen Keller was marked by her enormous powers of concentration, while the face of Mare

Winningham is merely cameo-pretty. A memory has been stolen. It takes a beauty in you to see the beauty in Helen Keller's face, while to cast the face of a Mare Winningham in the role is to suggest, powerfully, that one can come back from the depths unscathed. No small delusion is being sold here. Yet this is a minor instance in a worldwide, twenty-four-hour-a-day onslaught.

An onslaught that gathers momentum every twenty-four hours. Remember that what drew us to Las Vegas was a computer fair. One of these new computers does interesting things with photographs. You can put a photograph into the computer digitally. This means the photograph is in there without a negative or print, each element of the image stored separately. In the computer, you can change any element of the photograph you wish, replacing it or combining it with elements from other photographs. In other words, you can take composites of different photographs and put them into a new photograph of your own composition. Combine this with computer drawing, and you can touch up shadows that don't match. When it comes out of the computer the finished product bears no evidence of tampering with any negative. The possibilities for history books and news stories are infinite. Whole new histories can now be written. Events which never happened can be fully documented.

The neo-Nazis who are trying to convince people that the Holocaust never happened will be able to show the readers of their newsletter an Auschwitz of well-fed, happy people being watched over by kindly S.S. men while tending gardens. And they will be able to make the accusation that photographs of the *real* Auschwitz were created in a computer by manipulative Jews. The Soviet Union can rewrite Czechoslovakia and Afghanistan, the United States can rewrite Vietnam, and atomic weapons proponents can prove that the average resident of Hiroshima was unharmed by the blast. On a less sinister, but equally disruptive, level, the writers of business prospectuses and real-estate brochures can have a field day.

Needless to say, when any photograph can be processed this way then all photographs become suspect. It not only becomes easier to lie, it becomes far harder to tell the truth.

But why should this seem shocking when under the names of "entertainment" and "advertising" we've been filming history, and every facet of daily life, in just this way for nearly a century now? It shouldn't surprise us that the ethics of our entertainment have taken over, and that we are viewing reality itself as a form of entertainment. And, as entertainment, reality can be rewritten, transformed, played with, in any fashion.

These considerations place us squarely at the center of our world — and we have no choice, it's the only world there is anymore. *Electronic media has done for everyday reality what Einstein did for physics*: everything is shifting. Even the shifts are shifting. And a fact is not so crucial anymore, not so crucial as the process that turns a fact into an image. For we live now with images as much as facts, and the images seem to impart more life than facts *precisely because they are so capable of transmutation, of transcendence, able to transcend their sources and their uses*. And all the while the images goad us on, so that we become partly images ourselves, imitating the properties of images as we surround ourselves with images.

This is most blatant in our idea of "a vacation" — an idea only about 100 years old. To "vacation" is to enter an image. Las Vegas is only the most shrill embodiment of this phenomenon. People come here not so much to gamble (individual losses are comparatively light), nor for the glittery entertainment, but to step into an image, a daydream, a filmlike world where "everything" is promised. No matter that the Vegas definition of "everything" is severely limited, what thrills tourists is the sense of being surrounded in "real life" by the same images that they see on TV. But the same is true of the Grand Canyon, or Yellowstone National Park, or Yosemite, or Death Valley, or virtually any of our "natural" attractions. What with all their roads, telephones, bars, cable-TV motels, the visitors are carefully protected from having to *experience* the place. They view its image, they camp out in its image, ski down or climb up its image, take deep breaths of its image, let its image give them a tan. Or, when they tour the cities, they ride the quaint trolley cars of the city's image, they visit the Latin Quarter of its image, they walk across the Brooklyn Bridge of its image — our recreation is a *re*-creation of America into one big Disneyland.

And this is only one way we have stripped the very face of America of any content, any reality, concentrating only on its power as image. We also elect images, groom ourselves as images, make an image of our home, our car, and now, with aerobics, of our very bodies. For in the aerobics craze the flesh becomes a garment, susceptible to fashion. So it becomes less *our* flesh, though the exercise may make it more serviceable. It becomes "my" body, like "my" car, "my" house. What, within us, is saying "my"? What is transforming body into image? We shy away from asking. In this sense it can be said that after the age of about twenty-five we no longer *have* bodies anymore — we have possessions that are either more or less young, which we are constantly trying to transform and through which we try to breathe.

It's not that all this transformation of realities into un- or non- or supra-realities is "bad," but that it's unconscious, compulsive, reductive. We rarely make things more than they were; we simplify them into less. Though surely the process *could* — at least theoretically — go both ways. Or so India's meditators and Zen's monks say. But that would be to *increase* meaning, and we seem bent on the elimination of meaning. We're Reagan's Rangers, climbing a cliff that *is* a real cliff, except it's not the cliff we say it is, so that the meaning of both cliffs — not to mention of our act of climbing — is reduced.

As I look out onto a glowing city that is more than 400 years old but was built only during the last forty years, as I watch it shine in blinking neon in a desert that has seen the flash of atom bombs, it becomes more and more plain to me that America is at war with meaning. America is form opposed to content. Not just form *instead* of content. Form opposed. Often violently. There are few things resented so much among us as the suggestion that what we do *means*. It *means* something to watch so much TV. It *means* something to be obsessed with sports. It *means* something to vacation by indulging in images. It means something, and therefore it has consequences. Other cultures have argued over their meanings. We tend to deny that there is any such thing, insisting instead that what you see is what you get and that's *it*. All we're doing is having a *good time*, all we're doing is making a buck, all we're doing is enjoying the spectacle, we insist. So that when we export American culture what we are really exporting is an attitude toward content. Media is the American war on content with all the stops out, with meaning in utter rout, frightened nuances dropping their weapons as they run.

"Media is the history that forgives," my friend Dave Johnson told me on a drive through that same desert a few months later. We love to take a weekend every now and again and just *drive*. Maybe it started with reading *On the Road* when we were kids, or watching a great old TV show called *Route 66* about two guys who drove from town to town working at odd jobs and having adventures with intense women who, when asked who they were, might say (as one did), "Suppose I said I was the Queen of Spain?" Or maybe it was all those rock 'n' roll songs about "the road" — the road, where we can blast our tape-decks as loud as we want, and watch the world go by without having to touch it, a trip through the greatest hologram there is, feeling like neither boys nor men but both and something more, embodiments of some ageless, restless principle of movement rooted deep in our prehistory. All of which is to say that we're just as stuck with the compulsion to enter the image as anybody, and that we love the luxuries of fossil fuel just as much as any other red-blooded, thickheaded Americans.

Those drives are our favorite time to talk, and, again, America is our oldest flame. We never tire of speaking of her, nor of our other old girlfriends. For miles and miles of desert I thought of what Dave had said.

"Media is the history that forgives." A lovely way to put it, and quite un-Western. We Westerners tend to think in sets of opposites: good/bad, right/wrong, me/you, past/present. These sets are often either antagonistic (East/West, commie/capitalist, Christian/heathen) or they set up a duality that instantly calls out to be bridged (man/woman). But Dave's comment sidesteps the dualities and suggests something more complex: a lyrical impulse is alive somewhere in all this media obfuscation. It is the impulse to redeem the past — in his word, to *forgive* history — by presenting it as we would have most liked it to be.

It is one thing to accuse the media of lying. They are, and they know it, and they know we know, and we know they know that we know, and nothing changes. It is another to recognize the rampant lying shallowness of our media as a massive united longing for ... innocence? For a sheltered childlike state in which we need not know about our world or our past. We are so desperate for this that we are willing to accept ignorance as a substitute for innocence. For there can be no doubt anymore that this society *knowingly* accepts its ignorance as innocence — we have seen so much in the last twenty years that now we know what we *don't* see. Whenever a TV show or a movie or a news broadcast leaves out crucial realities for the sake of sentimentality, we pretty much understand the nature of what's been left out and why.

But American media *forgives* the emptiness and injustice of our daily life by presenting our daily life as innocent. Society, in turn, forgives American media for lying because if we accept the lie as truth then we needn't *do* anything, we needn't change.

I like Dave's line of thought because it suggests a motive — literally, a motive force — for these rivers of glop that stream from the screens and loudspeakers of our era. Because, contrary to popular belief, profit is *not* the motive. That seems a rash statement to make in the vicinity of Las Vegas, but the profit motive merely begs the question: *why* is it profitable? Profit, in media, is simply a way of measuring attention. Why does what we call "media" attract so much attention?

The answer is that it is otherwise too crippling for individuals to bear the strain of accepting the unbalanced, unrewarding, uninspiring existence that is advertised as "normal daily life" for most people who have to earn a living every day.

Do those words seem too strong? Consider: to go to a job you don't value in itself but for its paycheck, while your kids go to a school that is less and less able to educate them; a large percentage of your pay is taken by the government for defenses that don't defend, welfare that doesn't aid, and the upkeep of a government that is impermeable to the influence of a single individual; while you are caught in a value system that judges you by what you own, in a society where it is taken for granted now that children can't communicate with their parents, that old people have to be shut away in homes, and that no neighborhood is *really* safe; while the highest medical costs in the world don't prevent us from having one of the worst health records in the West (for instance, New York has a far higher infant mortality rate than Hong Kong), and the air, water, and supermarket food are filled with God-knows-what; and to have, at the end of a busy yet uneventful life, little to show for enduring all this but a comfortable home if you've "done well" enough; yet to *know* all along that you're living in the freest, most powerful country in the world, though you haven't had time to exercise much freedom and don't personally have any power — this is to be living a life of slow attrition and maddening contradictions.

Add to this a social style that values cheerfulness more than any other attribute, and then it is not so strange or shocking that the average American family watches six to eight hours of network television a day. It is a cheap and sanctioned way to partake of this world without having actually to live in it.

Certainly they don't watch so much TV because they're bored — there's far too much tension in their lives to call them bored, and, in fact, many of the products advertised on their favorite programs feature drugs to calm them down. Nor is it because they're stupid

— a people managing the most technically intricate daily life in history can hardly be written off as stupid; nor because they can't entertain themselves — they are not so different from the hundreds of generations of their forebears who entertained themselves very well as a matter of course. No, they are glued to the TV because one of the most fundamental messages of television is: "It's all right."

Every sitcom and drama says: "It's all right." Those people on the tube go through the same — if highly stylized — frustrations, and are exposed to the same dangers as we are, yet they reappear magically every week (every day on the soap operas) ready for more, always hopeful, always cheery, never questioning the fundamental premise that this is the way a great culture behaves and that all the harassments are the temporary inconveniences of a beneficent society. It's going to get even *better*, but even now *it's all right*. The commercials, the Hollywood movies, the universal demand in every television drama or comedy that no character's hope can ever be exhausted, combine in a deafening chorus of: *It's all right*.

As a screenwriter I have been in many a film production meeting, and not once have I heard any producer or studio executive say, "We have to lie to the public." What I have heard, over and over, is, "They have to leave the theater feeling good." This, of course, easily (though not always) translates into lying — into simplifying emotions and events so that "it's all right." You may measure how deeply our people know "it" is *not* all right, not at all, by how much money they are willing to pay to be ceaselessly told that it is. The more they feel it's not, the more they need to be told it is — hence Mr. Reagan's popularity.

Works that don't say "It's all right" don't get much media attention or make much money.

The culture itself is in the infantile position of needing to be assured, every day, all day, that this way of life is good for you. Even the most disturbing news is dispensed in the most reassuring package. As world news has gotten more and more disturbing, the trend in broadcast journalism has been to get more and more flimflam, to take it less seriously, to keep up the front of "It's really quite all right." This creates an enormous tension between the medium and its messages, because everybody knows that what's on the news is *not* all right. That is why such big money is paid to a newscaster with a clam, authoritative air who, by his presence alone, seems to resolve the contradictions of his medium. Walter Cronkite was the most popular newscaster in broadcast history because his very presence implied: "As long as I'm on the air, you can be sure that, no matter what I'm telling you, *it's still all right*."

Which is to say that the media has found it profitable to do the mothering of the mass psyche. But it's a weak mother. It cannot nurture. All it can do is say it's all right, tuck us in, and hope for the best.

Today most serious, creative people exhaust themselves in a sideline commentary on this state of affairs, a commentary that usually gets sucked up into the media and spewed back out in a format that says

"It's all right. What this guy's saying is quite all right, what this woman's singing is all right, all right." This is what "gaining recognition" virtually always means now in America: your work gets turned inside out so that its meaning becomes "It's all right."

Of course, most of what exist *to make media of*, to make images of, is more and more disorder. Media keeps saying, "It's all right" while being fixated upon the violent, the chaotic, and the terrifying. So the production of media becomes more and more schizoid, with two messages simultaneously being broadcast: "It's all right. We're dying. It's all right. We're all dying." The other crucial message — "We're dying" — runs right alongside *It's all right.*

Murder is the crux of much media "drama." But it's murder presented harmlessly, with trivial causes cited. Rare is the attempt, in all our thousands of murder dramas, to delve below the surface. We take for granted now, almost as an immutable principle of dramatic unity, that significant numbers of us want to kill significant numbers of the rest of us. And what are all the murders in our media but a way of saying "We are being killed, we are killing, we are dying"? Only a people dying and in the midst of death would need to see so much of it in such sanitized form *in order to make death harmless.* This is the way we choose to share our death.

Delete the word "entertainment" and say instead, North Americans devote an enormous amount of time to the ritual of sharing death. If this were recognized as a ritual, and if the deaths were shared with a respect for the realities and the mysteries of death, this might be a very useful thing to do. But there is no respect for death in our death-dependent media, there is only the compulsion to display death. As for the consumers, they consume these deaths like sugar pills. Their ritual goes on far beneath any level on which they'd be prepared to admit the word "ritual." So we engage in a ritual we pretend isn't happening, hovering around deaths that we say aren't real.

It is no coincidence that this practice has thrived while the Pentagon uses the money of these death watchers to create weapons for death on a scale that is beyond the powers of human imagination — the very same human imagination that is stunting itself by watching ersatz deaths, as though intentionally crippling its capacity to envision the encroaching dangers. It is possible that the Pentagon's process could not go on without the dulling effects of this "entertainment."

When we're not watching our screens, we're listening to music. And, of course, North Americans listen to love songs at every possible opportunity, through every possible orifice of media. People under the strain of such dislocating unrealities need to hear "I love you, I love you," as often as they can. "I love you" or "I used to love you" or "I ought to love you" or "I need to love you" or "I want to love you." It is the fashion of pop-music critics to discount the words for the style, forgetting that most of the world's cultures have had songs about *everything*, songs about work, about the sky, about death, about the gods, about getting up in the morning, about animals, about children, about eating, about dreams

— about everything, along with love. These were songs that everybody knew and sang. For a short time in the late sixties we moved toward such songs again, but that was a brief digression; since the First World War the music that most North Americans listen to has been a music of love lyrics that rarely go beyond adolescent yearnings. Either the song is steeped in the yearnings themselves, or it is saturated with a longing for the days when one could, shamelessly, feel like an adolescent. The beat has changed radically from decade to decade, but with brief exceptions that beat has carried the same pathetic load. (The beat, thankfully, has given us other gifts.)

It can't be over-emphasized that these are entertainments of a people whose basic imperative is the need not to think about their environment. The depth of their need may be measured by the hysterical popularity of this entertainment; it is also the measure of how little good it does them.

Media is not experience. In its most common form, media substitutes a fantasy of experience or (in the case of news) an abbreviation of experience for the living fact. But in our culture the absorption of media has become a substitute for experience. We absorb media, we don't live it — there is a vast psychological difference, and it is a difference that is rarely brought up.

For example, in the 1940, when one's environment was still one's *environment*, an experience to be lived instead of a media-saturation to be absorbed, teenagers like Elvis Presley and Jerry Lee Lewis didn't learn their music primarily from the radio. Beginning when they were small boys they sneaked over to the black juke joints of Louisiana and Mississippi and Tennessee, where they weren't supposed to go, and they listened and learned. When Lewis and Presley began recording, even though they were barely twenty they had tremendous authority because they had experience — a raw experience of crossing foreign boundaries, of streets and sounds and peoples, of the night-to-night learning of ways that could not be taught at home.

This is very different from young musicians now who learn from a product, not a living ground. Their music doesn't get to them till it's been sifted through elaborate corporate networks of production and distribution. It doesn't smack of the raw world that exists before "product" can even be thought of.

The young know this, of course. They sense the difference intensely, and often react to it violently. So white kids from suburban media culture invented slam dancing (jumping up and down and slamming into each other) while black kids from the South Bronx, who have to deal with realities far more urgent than media, were elaborating the astounding graces of break dancing.

Slam dancing was a dead end. Break dancing, coming from a living ground, goes out through media but becomes ultimately transformed into another living ground — the kids in the elementary school down the street in Santa Monica break dance. Which is to say, a grace has been added to their lives. A possibility of grace. With the vitality that comes from having originated from a living ground. The media here is taking its proper role as a channel, not as a world in itself. It's possible that these kids are being affected more in their bodies and their daily lives by the South Bronx subculture than by high-gloss films like *Gremlins* or *Indiana Jones and the Temple of Doom*. Even through all this static, life can speak to life.

Of course, break dancing inevitably gets hyped, and hence devalued, by the entertainment industry, the way Elvis Presley ended up singing "Viva Las Vegas" as that town's most glamorous headliner. He went from being the numinous son of a living ground to being the charismatic product of a media empire — the paradigm of media's power to transform the transformers. The town veritably glows in the dark with the strength of media's mystique.

We do not yet know what life *is* in a media environment. We have not yet evolved a contemporary culture that can supply the definition — or rather, supply the constellation of concepts in which that definition would live and grow. These seem such simple statements, but they are at the crux of the American dilemma now. An important aspect of this dilemma is that we've barely begun a body of thought and art which is focused on what is really *alive* in the ground of a media-saturated daily life. For culture always proceeds from two poles: one is the people of the land and the street; the other is the thinker. You see this most starkly in revolutions: the ground swell on the one hand, the thinker (the Jefferson, for instance) on the other. Or religiously, the ground swell of belief that is articulated by a Michelangelo or a Dante.

The two poles can exist without each other but they cannot be effective without each other.

Unless a body of thought connects with a living ground, there is no possibility that this era will discover itself within its cacophony and create, one day, a post-A.D. culture. It is ours to attempt the thought and seek the ground — for all of us exist between those poles. We are not only dying. We are living. And we are struggling to share our lives, which is all, finally, that "culture" means.

HOME IS WHERE THE *HAN* IS: A KOREAN-AMERICAN PERSPECTIVE ON THE LOS ANGELES UPHEAVALS

Elaine H. Kim

Elaine H. Kim teaches Asian American Studies at the University of California — Berkeley. She has written and edited a number of books on Asian American writers and artists, and she has been involved in the production of television documentaries on Asian women. The following selection originally appeared as a chapter in a collection of essays, *Reading Rodney King/ Reading Urban Uprising* (1993).

About half of the estimated $850 million in estimated material losses incurred during the Los Angles upheavals was sustained by a community no one seems to want to talk much about. Korean Americans in Los Angeles, suddenly at the front lines when violence came to the buffer zone they had been so precariously occupying, suffered profound damage to their means of livelihood. But my concern here is the psychic damage which, unlike material damage, is impossible to quantify.

I want to explore the questions of whether or not recovery is possible for Korean Americans, and what will become of our attempts to "become American" without dying of *han*. *Han* is a Korean word that means, loosely translated, the sorrow and anger that grow from the accumulated experiences of oppression. Although the word is frequently and commonly used by Koreans, the condition it describes is taken quite seriously. When people die of *han*, it is called dying of *hwabyong*, a disease of frustration and rage following misfortune.

Situated as we are on the border between those who have and those who have not, between predominantly Anglo and mostly African American and Latino communities, from our current interstitial position in the American discourse of race, many Korean Americans have trouble calling what happened in Los Angeles an "uprising." At the same time, we cannot quite say it was a "riot." So some of us have taken to calling it *sa-i-ku*, April 29, after the manner of naming other events in Korean history — 3.1 (*sam-il*) for March 1, 1919, when massive protests against Japanese colonial rule began in Korea; 6.25 (*yook-i-o*), or June 25, 1950, when the Korean War began; and 4.19 (*sa-il-ku*), or April 19, 1960, when the first student movement in the world to overthrow a government began in South Korea. The ironic similarity between 4.19 and 4.29 does not escape most Korean Americans.

Los Angeles Koreatown has been important to me, even though I visit only a dozen times a year. Before Koreatown sprang up during the last decade and a half, I used to hang around the fringes of Chinatown, although I knew that this habit was pure pretense. For me, knowing that Los Angeles Koreatown existed made a difference; one of my closest friends worked with the Black-Korean Alliance there, and I liked to think of it as a kind of "home" — however idealized and hypostatized — for the soul, an anchor, a potential refuge, a place in America where I could belong without ever being asked, "Who are you and what are you doing here? Where did you come from and when are you going back?"

Many of us watched in horror the destruction of Koreatown and the systematic targeting of Korean shops in South Central Los Angeles after the Rodney King verdict. Seeing those buildings in flames and those anguished Korean faces, I had the terrible thought that there would be no belonging and that we were, just as I had always suspected, a people destined to carry our *han* around with us wherever we went in the world. The destiny (*p'aljja*) that had spelled centuries of extreme suffering from invasion, colonization, war, and national division had smuggled itself into the U.S. with our baggage.

AFRICAN AMERICAN AND KOREAN AMERICAN CONFLICT

As someone whose social consciousness was shaped by the African American-led civil rights movement of the 1960s, I felt that I was watching our collective dreams for a just society disintegrating, cast aside as naive and irrelevant in the bitter and embattled 1990s. It was the courageous African American women and men of the 1960s who had redefined the meaning of

"American," who had first suggested that a person like me could reject the false choice between being treated as a perpetual foreigner in my own birthplace, on the one hand, and relinquishing my identity for someone else's ill-fitting and impossible Anglo American one on the other. Thanks to them, I began to discern how institutional racism works and why Korea was never mentioned in my world-history textbooks. I was able to see how others besides Koreans had been swept aside by the dominant culture. My American education offered nothing about Chicanos or Latinos, and most of what I was taught about African and Native Americans was distorted to justify their oppression and vindicate their oppressors.

I could hardly believe my ears when, during the weeks immediately following *sa-i-ku*, I heard African American community leaders suggesting that Korean American merchants were foreign intruders deliberately trying to stifle African American economic development, when I knew that they had bought those liquor stores at five times gross receipts from African American owners, who had previously bought them at two times gross receipts from Jewish owners after Watts. I saw anti-Korean flyers that were being circulated by African American political candidates and read about South Central residents petitioning against the reestablishment of swap meets, groups of typically Korean immigrant-operated market stalls. I was disheartened with Latinos who related the pleasure they felt while looting Korean stores that they believed "had it coming" and who claimed that it was because of racism that more Latinos were arrested during *sa-i-ku* than Asian Americans. And I was filled with despair when I read about Chinese Americans wanting to dissociate themselves from us. According to one Chinese American reporter assigned to cover Asian American issues for a San Francisco daily, Chinese and Japanese American shopkeepers, unlike Koreans, always got along fine with African Americans in the past. "Suddenly," admitted another Chinese American, "I am scared to be Asian. More specifically, I am afraid to be mistaken for Korean." I was enraged when I overheard European Americans discussing the conflicts as if they were watching a dogfight or a boxing match. The situation reminded me of the Chinese film "Raise the Red Lantern," in which we never see the husband's face. We only hear his mellifluous voice as he benignly admonishes his four wives not to fight among themselves. He can afford to be kind and pleasant because the structure that pits his wives against each other is so firmly in place that he need never sully his hands or even raise his voice.

BATTLEGROUND LEGACY

Korean Americans are squeezed between black and white and also between U.S. and South Korean political agendas. Opportunistic American and South Korean presidential candidates toured the burnt ruins, posing for the television cameras but delivering nothing of substance to the victims. Like their U.S. counterparts, South Korean news media seized upon *sa-i-ku*, featuring sensational stories that depicted the problem as that of savage African Americans attacking innocent Koreans for no reason. To give the appearance of authenticity, Seoul newspapers even published articles using the names of Korean Americans who did not in fact write them.

Those of us who chafe at being asked whether we are Chinese or Japanese as if there were no other possibilities or who were angered when the news media sought Chinese and Japanese but not Korean American views during *sa-i-ku* are sensitive to an invisibility that seems particular to us. To many Americans, Korea is but the gateway to or the bridge between China and Japan, or a crossroads of major Asian conflicts.

It can certainly be said that, although little known or cared about in the Western world, Korea has been a perennial battleground. Besides the Mongols and the Manchus, there were the *Yŏjin* (Jurched), the *Koran* (Khitan), and the *Waega* (Wäkö) invaders. In relatively recent years, there was the war between China and Japan that ended in 1895 and the war between Japan and Russia in 1905; both of which were fought on Korean soil and resulted in extreme suffering for the Korean people. Japan's 36 years of brutal colonial rule ended with the U.S. and what was then the Soviet Union dividing the country in half at the 38th parallel. Thus, Korea was turned into a Cold War territory that ultimately became a battleground for world superpowers during the conflict of 1950-53.

BECOMING AMERICAN

One of the consequences of war, colonization, national division, and superpower economic and cultural domination has been the migration of Koreans to places like Los Angeles, where they believed their human rights would be protected by law. After all, they had received U.S.-influenced political educations. They started learning English in the seventh grade. They all knew the story of the poor boy from Illinois who became president. They all learned that the U.S. Constitution and Bill of Rights protected the common people from violence and injustice. But they who grew up in Korea watching “Gunsmoke,” “Night Rider,” and “McGyver” dubbed in Korean were not prepared for the black, brown, red, and yellow America they encountered when they disembarked at the Los Angeles International Airport. They hadn’t heard that there is no equal justice in the U.S. They had to learn about American racial hierarchies. They did not realize that, as immigrants of color, they would never attain political voice or visibility but would instead be used to uphold the inequality and the racial hierarchy they had no part in creating.

Most of the newcomers had underestimated the communication barriers they would face. Like the Turkish workers in Germany described in John Berger and Jean Mohr’s *A Seventh Man*, their toil amounted to only a pile of gestures and the English they tried to speak changed and turned against them as they spoke it. Working 14 hours a day, six or seven days a week, they rarely came into sustained contact with English-speaking Americans and almost never had time to study English. Not feeling at ease with English, they did not engage in informal conversations easily with non-Koreans and were hated for being curt and rude. They did not attend churches or do business in banks or other enterprises where English was required. Typically, the immigrant, small-business owners utilized unpaid family labor instead of hiring people from local communities. Thanks to Eurocentric American cultural practices, they knew little or nothing good about African Americans or Latinos, who in turn and for similar reasons knew little or nothing good about them. At the same time, Korean shopowners in South Central and Koreatown were affluent compared with the impoverished residents, whom they often exploited as laborers or looked down upon as fools with an aversion to hard work. Most Korean immigrants did not even know that they were among the many direct beneficiaries of the African American-led civil rights movement, which helped pave the way for the 1965 immigration reforms that made their immigration possible.

Korean-immigrant views, shaped as they were by U.S. cultural influences and official, anticommunist, South Korean education, differed radically from those of many poor people in the communities Korean immigrants served: unaware of the shameful history of oppression of nonwhite immigrants and other people of color in the U.S., they regarded themselves as having arrived in a meritocratic "land of opportunity" where a person's chances for success are limited only by individual lack of ability or diligence. Having left a homeland where they foresaw their talents and hard work going unrecognized and unrewarded, they were desperate to believe that the "American dream" of social and economic mobility through hard work was within their reach.

SA-I-KU

What they experienced on 29 and 30 April was a baptism into what it really means for a Korean to "become American" in the 1990s. In South Korea, there is no 911, and no one really expects a fire engine or police car if there is trouble. Instead, people make arrangements with friends and family for emergencies. At the same time, guns are not part of Korean daily life. No civilian in South Korea can own a gun. Guns are the exclusive accoutrement of the military and police who enforce order for those who rule the society. When the Korean Americans in South Central and Koreatown dialed 911, nothing happened. When their stores and homes were being looted and burned to the ground, they were left completely alone for three horrifying days. How betrayed they must have felt by what they had believed was a democratic system that protects its people from violence. Those who trusted the government to protect them lost everything; those who took up arms after waiting for help for two days were able to defend themselves. It was as simple as that. What they had to learn was that, as in South Korea, protection in the U.S. is by and large for the rich and powerful. If there were a choice between Westwood and Koreatown, it is clear that Koreatown would have to be sacrificed. The familiar concept of privilege for the rich and powerful would have been easy for the Korean immigrant to grasp if only those exhortations about democracy and equality had not obfuscated the picture. Perhaps they should have relied even more on whatever they brought with them from Korea instead of fretting over trying to understand what was going on around them here. That Koreatown became a battleground does seem like the further playing out of a tragic legacy that has followed them across oceans and continents. The difference is that this was a battle between the poor and disenfranchised and the invisible rich, who were being protected by a layer of clearly visible Korean American human shields in a battle on the buffer zone.

This difference is crucial. Perhaps the legacy is not one carried across oceans and continents but one assumed immediately upon arrival, not the curse of being Korean but the initiation into becoming American, which requires that Korean Americans take on this country's legacy of five centuries of racial violence and inequality, of divide and rule, of privilege for the rich and oppression of the poor. Within this legacy, they have been assigned a place on the front lines. Silenced by those who possess the power to characterize and represent, they are permitted to speak only to reiterate their acceptance of this role.

SILENCING THE KOREAN AMERICAN VOICE

Twelve years ago, in Kwangju, South Korea, hundreds of civilians demonstrating for constitutional reform and free elections were murdered by U.S. -supported and -equipped South Korean elite paratroopers. Because I recorded it and played it over and over again, searching for a sign or a clue, I remember clearly how what were to me heartrendingly tragic events were represented in the U.S. news media. For a few fleeting moments, images of unruly crowds of alien-looking Asians shouting unintelligible words and phrases and wearing white headbands inscribed with unintelligible characters flickered across the screen. The Koreans were made to seem like insane people from another planet. The voice in the background stated simply that there were massive demonstrations but did not explain what the protests were about. Nor was a single Korean ever given an opportunity to speak to the camera.

The next news story was about demonstrations for democracy in Poland. The camera settled on individuals' faces which one by one filled the screen as each man or woman was asked to explain how he or she felt. Each Polish person's words were translated in a voice-over or subtitle. Solidarity leader Lech Walesa, who was allowed to speak often, was characterized as a heroic human being with whom all Americans could surely identify personally. Polish Americans from New York and Chicago to San Francisco, asked in man-on-the-street interviews about their reactions, described the canned hams and blankets they were sending to Warsaw.

This was for me a lesson in media representation, race, and power politics. It is a given that Americans are encouraged by our ideological apparatuses to side with our allies (here, the Polish resisters and the anti-communist South Korean government) against our enemies (here, the communist Soviet Union and protesters against the South Korean government). But visual-media racism helps craft and reinforce our identification with Europeans and whites while distancing us from fearsome and alien Asiatic hordes.

In March of last year, when two delegates from North Korea visited the Bay Area to participate in community-sponsored talks on Korean reunification, about 800 people from the Korean American community attended. The meeting was consummately newsworthy, since it was the first time in history that anyone from North Korea had ever been in California for more than 24 hours just passing through. The event was discussed for months in the Korean-language media — television, radio, and newspapers. Almost every Korean-speaking person in California knew about it. Although we sent press releases to all the commercial and public radio and television stations and to all the Bay Area newspapers, not a single mainstream media outfit covered the event. However, whenever there was an African American boycott of a Korean store or whenever conflict surfaced between Korean and African Americans, community leaders found a dozen microphones from all the main news media shoved into their faces, as if they were the president's press secretary making an official public pronouncement. Fascination with interethnic conflicts is rooted in the desire to excuse or minimize white racism by buttressing the mistaken notion that all human beings are "naturally" racist, and when Korean and African Americans allow themselves to be distracted by these interests, their attention is deflected from the social hierarchies that give racism its destructive power.

Without a doubt, the U.S. news media played a major role in exacerbating the damage and ill will toward Korean Americans, first by spotlighting tensions between African Americans and Koreans above all efforts to work together and as opposed to many other newsworthy events in these two communities, and second by exploiting racist stereotypes of Koreans as unfathomable aliens, this time wielding guns on rooftops and allegedly firing wildly into crowds. In news programs and on talk shows, African and Korean American tensions were discussed by blacks and whites, who pointed to these tensions as the main cause of the uprising. I heard some European Americans railing against rude and exploitative Korean merchants for ruining peaceful race relations for everyone else. Thus, Korean Americans were used to deflect attention from the racism they inherited and the economic injustice and poverty that had been already well woven into the fabric of American life, as evidenced by a judicial system that could allow not only the Korean store owner who killed Latasha Harlins but also the white men who killed Vincent Chin and the white police who beat Rodney King to go free, while Leonard Peltier still languishes in prison.

As far as I know, neither the commercial nor the public news media has mentioned the many Korean and African American attempts to improve relations, such as joint church services, joint musical performances and poetry readings, Korean merchant donations to African American community and youth programs, African American volunteer teachers in classes for Korean immigrants studying for citizenship examinations, or Korean translations of African American history materials.

While Korean immigrants were preoccupied with the mantra of day-to-day survival, Korean Americans had no voice, no political presence whatsoever in American life. When they became the targets of violence in Los Angeles, their opinions and views were hardly solicited except as they could be used in the already-constructed mainstream discourse on race relations, which is a sorry combination of blaming the African American and Latino victims for their poverty and scapegoating the Korean Americans as robotic aliens who have no "real" right to be here in the first place and therefore deserve whatever happens to them.

THE *NEWSWEEK* EXPERIENCE

In this situation, I felt compelled to respond when an editor from the "My Turn" section of *Newsweek* magazine asked for a 1000-word personal essay. Hesitant because I was given only a day and a half to write the piece, not enough time in light of the vastness of American ignorance about Koreans and Korean Americans, I decided to do it because I thought I could not be made into a sound bite or a quote contextualized for someone else's agenda.

I wrote an essay accusing the news media of using Korean Americans and tensions between African and Korean Americans to divert attention from the roots of racial violence in the U.S. I asserted that these lie not in the Korean-immigrant-owned corner store situated in a community ravaged by poverty and police violence, but reach far back into the corridors of corporate and government offices in Los Angeles, Sacramento, and Washington, D.C. I suggested that Koreans and African Americans were kept ignorant about each other by educational and media institutions that erase or distort their experiences and perspectives. I tried to explain how racism had kept my parents from ever really becoming Americans, but that having been born here, I considered myself American and wanted to believe in the possibility of an American dream.

The editor of "My Turn" did everything he could to frame my words with his own viewpoint. He faxed his own introductory and concluding paragraphs that equated Korean merchants with cowboys in the Wild West and alluded to Korean/African American hatred. When I objected, he told me that my writing style was not crisp enough and that as an experienced journalist, he could help me out. My confidence wavered, but ultimately I rejected his editing. Then he accused me of being overly sensitive, confiding that I had no need to be defensive — because his wife was a Chinese American. Only after I had decided to withdraw the piece did he agree to accept it as I wrote it.

Before I could finish congratulating myself on being able to resist silencing and the kind of decontextualization I was trying to describe in the piece, I started receiving hate mail. Some of it was addressed directly to me, since I had been identified as a University of California faculty member, but most of it arrived in bundles, forwarded by *Newsweek*. Hundreds of letters came from all over the country, from Florida to Washington state and from Massachusetts to Arizona. I was unprepared for the hostility expressed in most of the letters. Some people sent the article, torn from the magazine and covered with angry, red-inked obscenities scratched across my picture. "You should see a good doctor," wrote someone from Southern California, "you have severe problems in thinking, reasoning, and adjusting to your environment."

A significant proportion of the writers, especially those who identified themselves as descendants of immigrants from Eastern Europe, wrote *Newsweek* that they were outraged, sickened, disgusted, appalled, annoyed, and angry at the magazine for providing an arena for the paranoid, absurd, hypocritical, racist, and childish views of a spoiled, ungrateful, whining, bitching, un-American bogus faculty member who should be fired or die when the next California earthquake dumps all of the "so-called people of color" into the Pacific Ocean.

I was shocked by the profound ignorance of many writers' assumptions about the experiences and perspectives of American people of color in general and Korean and other Asian Americans in particular. Even though my essay revealed that I was born in the U.S. and that my parents had lived in the U.S. for more than six decades, I was viewed as a foreigner without the right to say anything except words of gratitude and praise about America. The letters also provided some evidence of the dilemma Korean Americans are placed in by those who assume that we are aliens who should "go back" and at the same time berate us for not rejecting "Korean-American identity" for "American identity."

> How many Americans migrate to Korea? If you are so disenchanted, Korea is still there. Why did you ever leave it? Sayonara.

> Ms. Kim appears to have a personal axe to grind with this country that has given her so much freedom and opportunity. . . . I should suggest that she move to Korea, where her children will learn all they ever wanted about that country's history.

> [Her] whining about the supposedly racist U.S. society is just a mask for her own acute inferiority complex. If she is so dissatisfied with the United States why doesn't she vote with her feet and leave? She can get the hell out and return to her beloved Korea — her tribal afinity [*sic*] where her true loyalty and consciousness lies [*sic*].

> You refer to yourself as a Korean American and yet you have lived all your life in the United States . . . you write about racism in this country and yet you are the biggest racist by your own written words. If you cannot accept the fact that you are an American, maybe you should be living your life in Korea.

> My stepfather and cousin risked their lives in the country where your father is buried to ensure the ideals of our country would remain. So don't expect to find a sympathetic ear for your pathetic whining.

Many of the letter writers assumed that my family had been the "scum" of Asia and that I was a college teacher only because of American justice and largesse. They were furious that I did not express gratitude for being saved from starvation in Asia and given the opportunity to flourish, no doubt beyond my wildest dreams, in America.

> Where would she be if her parents had not migrated to the United States? For a professor at Berkeley University [*sic*] to say the American dream is only an empty promise is ludicrous. Shame, shame, shame on Elaine!

> [Her father and his family] made enough money in the USA to ship his corpse home to Korea for burial. Ms. Kim herself no doubt has a guaranteed life income as a professor paid by California taxpayers. Wouldn't you think that she might say kind things about the USA instead of whining about racism?

At the same time some letters blamed me for expecting "freedom and opportunity":

> It is wondrous that folks such as you find truth in your paranoia. No one ever promised anything to you or your parents.

Besides providing indications of how Korean Americans are regarded, the letters revealed a great deal about how American identity is thought of. One California woman explained that although her grandparents were Irish immigrants, she was not an Irish American, because "if you are not with us, you are against us." A Missouri woman did not seem to realize that she was conflating race and nationality and confusing "nonethnic" and "nonracial," by which she seems to have meant "white," with "American." And, although she insists that it is impossible to be both "black" and "American," she identifies herself at the outset as a "white American."

> I am a white American. I am proud to be an American. You cannot be black, white, Korean, Chinese, Mexican, German, French, or English or any other and still be an American. Of course the culture taught in schools is strictly American. That's where we are and if you choose to learn another [culture] you have the freedom to settle there. You cannot be a Korean American which assumes you are not ready to be an AMERICAN. Do you get my gist?

The suggestion that more should be taught in U.S. schools about America's many immigrant groups and people of color prompted many letters in defense of Western civilization against non-Western barbarism:

> You are dissatisfied with current school curricula that excludes Korea. Could it possibly be because Korea and Asia for that matter has [*sic*] not had . . . a noticeable impact on the shaping of Western culture, and Korea has had unfortunately little culture of its own?

> Who cares about Korea, Ms. Kim? . . . And what enduring contributions has the Black culture, both here in the US and on the continent contributed to the world, and mankind? I'm from a culture, Ms. Kim, who put a man on the moon 23 years ago, who established medical schools to train doctors to perform open heart surgery, and . . . who created a language of music so that musicians, from Beethoven to the Beatles, could easily touch the world with their brilliance forever and ever and ever. Perhaps the dominant culture, whites obviously, "swept aside Chicanos . . . Latinos . . . African-Americans . . . Koreans," because they haven't contributed anything that made — be mindful of the cliche — a world of difference?

> Koreans' favorite means of execution is decapitation . . . Ms. Kim,

> and others like her, came here to escape such injustice. Then they whine at riots to which they have contributed by their own fanning of flames of discontent . . . Yes! Let us all study more about Oriental culture! Let us put matters into proper perspective.

> Fanatical multiculturalists like you expect a country whose dominant culture has been formed and influenced by Europe. . . , nearly 80% of her population consisting of persons whose ancestry is European, to include the history of every ethnic group who has ever lived here. I truly feel sorry for you. You and your bunch need to realize that white Americans are not racists. . . . We would love to get along, but not at the expense of our own culture and heritage.

> Kim's axe-to-grind confirms the utter futility of race-relations — the races were never meant to live together. We don't get along and never will. . . . Whats [*sic*] needed is to divide the United States up along racial lines so that life here can finally become livable.

What seemed to anger some people the most was their idea that, although they worked hard, people of color were seeking handouts and privileges because of their race, and the thought of an ungrateful Asian American siding with African Americans, presumably against whites, was infuriating. How dare I "bite the hand that feeds" me by siding with the champion "whiners who cry 'racism'" because to do so is the last refuge of the "terminally incompetent"?

> The racial health in this country won't improve until minorities stop erecting "me first" barriers and strive to be Americans, not African-Americans or Asian-Americans expecting privileges.

> Ms. Kim wants preferential treatment that immigrants from Greece-to-Sweden have not enjoyed. . . . Even the Chinese . . . have not created any special problems for themselves or other Americans. Soon those folk are going to express their own resentments to the insatiable demands of the Blacks and other colored peoples, including the wetbacks from Mexico who sneak into this country then pilfer it for all they can.

> The Afroderived citizens of Los Angeles and the Asiatic derivatives were not suffering a common imposition. . . . The Asiatics are trying to build their success. The Africans are sucking at the teats of entitlement.

As is usual with racists, most of the writers of these hate letters saw only themselves in their notions about Korea, America, Korean Americans, African Americans. They felt that their own sense of American identity was being threatened and that they were being blamed as individuals for U.S. racism. One man, adept at manipulating various fonts on his word processor, imposed his preconceptions on my words:

> Let me read between the lines of your little hate message:
>
> . . . "The roots . . . stretch far back into the corridors of corporate and government offices in Los Angeles, Sacramento, and Washington, D.C."
>
> All white America and all American institutions are to blame for racism.
>
> . . . "I still want to believe the promise is real."

> I have the savvy to know that the American ideals of freedom and justice are a joke but if you want to give me what I want I'm willing to make concessions.
>
> Ms. Kim. . . . if you want to embody the ignorant, the insecure, and the emotionally immature, that's your right! Just stop preaching hate and please, please, quit whining.
>
> Sincerely, A proud White-American teaching my children not to be prejudicial

Especially since my essay had been subdued and intensely personal, I had not anticipated the fury it would provoke. I never thought that readers would write over my words with their own. The very fact that I used words, and English words at that, particularly incensed some: one letter writer complained about my use of words and phrases like "manifestation" and "zero-sum game," and "suzerain relationship," which is the only way to describe Korea's relationship with China during the T'ang Dynasty. "Not more than ten people in the USA know what [these words] mean," he wrote. "You are on an ego trip." I wondered if it made him particularly angry that an Asian American had used those English words, or if he would make such a comment to George Will or Jane Bryant Quinn.

Clearly I had encountered part of America's legacy, the legacy that insists on silencing certain voices and erasing certain presences, even if it means deportation, internment, and outright murder. I should not have been surprised by what happened in Koreatown or by the ignorance and hatred expressed in the letters to *Newsweek*, any more than African Americans should have been surprised by the Rodney King verdict. Perhaps the news media, which constituted *sa-i-ku* as news, as an extraordinary event in no way continuous with our everyday lives, made us forget for a moment that as people of color many of us simultaneously inhabit two Americas: the America of our dreams and the America of our experience.

Who among us does not cling stubbornly to the America of our dreams, the promise of a multicultural democracy where our cultures and our differences might be affirmed instead of distorted in an effort to destroy us?

After *sa-i-ku*, I was able to catch glimpses of this America of my dreams because I received other letters that expressed another American legacy. Some people identified themselves as Norwegian or Irish Americans interested in combating racism. Significantly, while most of the angry mail had been sent not to me but to *Newsweek*, almost all of the sympathetic mail, particularly the letters from African Americans, came directly to me. Many came from Korean Americans who were glad that one of their number had found a vehicle for self-expression. Others were from Chinese and Japanese Americans who wrote that they had had similar experiences and feelings. Several were written in shaky longhand by women fervently wishing for peace and understanding among people of all races. A Native American from Nashville wrote a long description of cases of racism against African, Asian, and

Native Americans in the U.S. criminal-justice system. A large number of letters came from African Americans, all of them supportive and sympathetic — from judges and professors who wanted better understanding between Africans and Koreans to poets and laborers who scribbled their notes in pencil while on breaks at work. One man identified himself as a Los Angeles African American whose uncle had married a Korean woman. He stated that as a black man in America, he knew what other people feel when they face injustice. He ended his letter apologizing for his spelling and grammar mistakes and asking for materials to read on Asian Americans. The most touching letter I received was written by a prison inmate who had served twelve years of a 35-to-70-year sentence for armed robbery during which no physical injuries occurred. He wrote:

> I've been locked in these prisons going on 12 years now . . . and since being here I have studied fully the struggles of not just blacks, but all people of color. I am a true believer of helping "your" people "first," but also the helping of all people no matter where there at or the color of there skin. But I must be truthful, my struggle and assistance is truly on the side of people of color like ourselves. But just a few years ago I didn't think like this.
>
> I thought that if you wasn't black, then you was the enemy, but . . . many years of this prison madness and much study and research changed all of this. . . . [I]t's not with each other, blacks against Koreans or Koreans against blacks. No, this is not what it's about. Our struggle(s) are truly one in the same. What happened in L.A. during the riot really hurt me, because it was no way that blacks

> was suppose to do the things to your people, my people (Koreans) that they did. You're my sister, our people are my people. Even though our culture may be somewhat different, and even though we may worship our God(s) different . . . white-Amerikkka [doesn't] separate us. They look at us all the same. Either you're white, or you're wrong. . . . I'm just writing you to let you know that, you're my sister, your people's struggle are my people's struggle.

This is the ground I need to claim now for Korean American resistance and recovery, so that we can become American without dying of *han*.

Although the sentiments expressed in these letters seemed to break down roughly along racial lines — that is, all writers who were identifiably people of color wrote in support — and one might become alarmed at the depth of the divisions they imply, I like to think that I have experienced the desire of many Americans, especially Americans of color, to do as Rodney King pleaded on the second day of *sa-i-ku*: "We're all stuck here for awhile. . . . Let's try to work it out."

In my view, it's important for us to think about *all* of what Rodney King said and not just the words "we all can get along," which have been depoliticized and transformed into a Disneyesque catchphrase for Pat Boone songs and roadside billboards in Los Angeles. It seems to me the emphasis is on the being "stuck here for awhile" together as we await "our day in court."

Like the African American man who wrote from prison, the African American man who had been brutally beaten by white police might have felt the desire to "love everybody," but he had to amend — or rectify — that wish. He had to speak last about loving "people of color." The impulse to "love everybody" was there, but the conditions were not right. For now, the most practical and progressive agenda may be people of color trying to "work it out."

FINDING COMMUNITY THROUGH NATIONAL CONSCIOUSNESS

The place where Korean and American legacies converge for Korean Americans is the exhortation to "go home to where you belong."

One of the letters I received was from a Korean American living in Chicago. He had read a translation of my essay in a Korean language newspaper. "Although you were born in the U.S.A," he wrote, noticing what none of the white men who ordered me to go back to "my" country had, "your ethnical background and your complexion belong to Korea. It is time to give up your U.S. citizenship and go to Korea."

Some ruined merchants are claiming that they will pull up stakes and return to Korea, but I know that this is not possible for most of them. Even if their stores had not been destroyed, even if they were able to sell their businesses and take the proceeds to Korea, most of them would not have enough to buy a home or business there, since both require total cash up front. Neither would they be able to find work in the society they left behind because it is plagued by recession, repression, and fierce economic competition.

Going back to Korea. The dream of going back to Korea fed the spirit of my father, who came to Chicago in 1926 and lived in the United States for 63 years, during which time he never became a U.S. citizen, at first because the law did not allow it and later because he did not want to. He kept himself going by believing that he would return to Korea in triumph one day. Instead, he died in Oakland at 88. Only his remains returned to Korea, where we buried him in accordance with his wishes.

Hasn't the dream of going back home to where you belong sustained most of America's unwanted at one time or another, giving meaning to lives of toil and making it possible to endure other people's hatred and rejection? Isn't the attempt to find community through national consciousness natural for people refused an American identity because racism does not give them that choice?

Korean national consciousness, the resolve to resist and fight back when threatened with extermination, was all that could be called upon when the Korean Americans in Los Angeles found themselves abandoned. They joined together to guard each other's means of livelihood with guns, relying on Korean-language radio and newspapers to communicate with and help each other. On the third day after the outbreak of violence, more than 30,000 Korean Americans gathered for a peace march in downtown L.A. in what was perhaps the largest and most quickly organized mass mobilization in Asian American history. Musicians in white, the color of mourning, beat traditional Korean drums in sorrow, anger, and celebration of community, a call to arms like a collective heartbeat. I believe that the mother of Edward Song Lee, the Los Angeles-born college student mistaken for a looter and shot to death in the streets, has been able to persevere in great part because of the massive outpouring of sympathy expressed by the Korean-American community that shared and understood her *han*.

I have been critical lately of cultural nationalism as detrimental to Korean Americans, especially Korean American women, because it operates on exclusions and fosters intolerance and uniformity of thought while stifling self-criticism and encouraging sacrifice, even to the point of suicide. But *sa-i-ku* makes me think again: what remains for those who are left to stand alone? If Korean Americans refuse to be victims or political pawns in the U.S. while rejecting the exhortation that we go back to Korea where we belong, what will be our weapons of choice?

In the darkest days of Japanese colonial rule, even after being stripped of land and of all economic means of survival, Koreans were threatened with total erasure when the colonizers rewrote Korean history, outlawed the Korean language, forced the subjugated people to worship the Japanese emperor, and demanded that they adopt Japanese names. One of the results of these cultural-annihilation policies was Korean's fierce insistence on the sanctity of Korean national identity that persists to this day. In this context, it is not difficult to understand why nationalism has been the main refuge of Korean and Korean Americans.

While recognizing the potential dangers of nationalism as a

weapon, I for one am not ready to respond to the antiessentialists' call to relinquish my Korean American identity. It is easy enough for the French and Germans to call for a common Europen identity and an end to nationalisms, but what of the peoples suppressed and submerged while France and Germany exercised their national prerogatives? I am mindful of the argument that the resurgence of nationalism in Europe is rooted in historical and contemporary political and economic inequality among the nations of Europe. Likewise, I have noticed that many white Americans do not like to think of themselves as belonging to a race, even while thinking of people of color almost exclusively in terms of race. In the same way, many men think of themselves as "human beings" and of women as the ones having a gender. Thus crime, small businesses, and all Korean-African American interactions are seen and interpreted through the lens of race in the same dominant culture that angrily rejects the use of the racial lens for viewing yellow/white or black/white interactions and insists suddenly that we are all "American" whenever we attempt to assert our identity as people of color. It is far easier for Anglo Americans to call for an end to cultural nationalisms than for Korean Americans to give up national consciousness, which makes it possible to survive the vicious racism that would deny our existence as either Korean Americans or Americans.

Is there anything of use to us in Korean nationalism? During one thousand years of Chinese suzerainty, the Korean ruling elite developed a philosophy called *sadaejui*, or reliance of the weak on the strong. In direct opposition to this way of thought is what is called *jaju* or *juche sasang*, or self-determination. Both *sadaejui* and *juche sasang* are ways of dealing with unequal power relationships and resisting the transformation of one's homeland into a battlefield for others, but *sadaejui* has never worked any better for Koreans than it has for any minority group in America. *Juche sasang*, on the other hand, has the kind of oppositional potential needed in the struggle against silence and invisibility. From Korean national consciousness, we can recover this fierce refusal to accept subjugation, which is the first step in the effort to build community, so that we can work with others to challenge the forces that would have us annihilate each other instead of our mutual oppression.

What is clear is that we cannot "become American" without dying of *han* unless we think about community in new ways. Self-determination does not mean living alone. At least for now, that may mean mining the rich and haunted lode of Korean national consciousness while we struggle to understand how our fate is entwined with the fate of others lying prostrate before the triumphal procession of the winners of History. During the past fifteen years or so, many young Korean nationalists have been studying the legacies of colonialism and imperialism that they share with peoples in many Asian, African, and Latin American nations. At the same time that we take note of this work, we can also try to understand how nationalism and feminism can be worked together to demystify the limitations and reductiveness of each as a weapon of empowerment. If Korean national consciousness is ever to be such a weapon for us, we must use it to create a new kind of nationalism-in-internationalism to help us call forth a culture of survival and recovery, so that our *han* might be released and we might be freed to dream fiercely of different possibilities.

The 1980s Caused Cultural and Economic Decline

Cornel West

Paradigmatic public intellectual, professor of Afro-American studies and the philosophy of religion, also honorary co-chair of the Democratic Socialists of America. Author of best-selling *Race Matters* (1993).

> "Instead of reviving traditional values, . . . the 1980s have ironically yielded a populace that is suspicious of the common good and addicted to narrow pleasures."

The 1980s were not simply a decade of glitz and greed. More important, they ushered in a new era of American history — the triumphant conservatism of Ronald Reagan, Rambo and retrenchment. The Reagan revolution was a full-blown ideological response to the anemic liberalism of the Jimmy Carter presidency that faltered in the face of runaway inflation, sluggish economic growth, the Iranian hostage crisis and the relative erosion of America's place in the global economy. The Rambo mentality harked back to a gunfighter readiness to do battle with an "evil" empire at nearly any cost. And the unapologetic retrenchment took the form of making people more comfortable with their prejudices and reducing public focus on the disadvantaged. The '80s discouraged a serious national conversation on the deep problems confronting us.

Laissez-Faire Capitalism

For the first time since the 1920s, the political Right — along with highly organized conservative corporate and bank elites — boldly attempted to reform American society. The aim of Reaganomics — couched in the diverse languages of supply-siders (Arthur Laffer), single-minded monetarists (Paul Volcker) and budget balancers (Alan Greenspan) — was to give new life to the utopian ideology of laissez-faire capitalism. This ideology cast high taxes, regulation and welfare assistance to the poor as the major impediments to economic growth and prosperity. Low taxes, deregulation and cutbacks in liberal social programs were viewed as a means to curtail inflation and generate an economic boom.

The decade brought us the largest peacetime military buildup in American history (about 28 percent of the federal budget in 1988!); it brought us the shortsighted choices of highly compensated corporate executives to consume, acquire and merge rather than invest, research and innovate. Together these developments caused high levels of public and private debt and the starvation of the public sector. There was little money for roads, railways, community development, housing, education, neighborhood improvement and, above all, decent-paying jobs for those displaced by industrial flight.

In the 1980s, the expansion of unfettered markets produced great wealth for the top 1 percent of the population, impressive income for the top 20 percent and significant decline in real wages for the bottom 40 percent. For example, the top 1 percent owned 44 percent of the household net wealth in 1929 and 36 percent in 1989 (in 1976, it dropped to 20 percent). By 1989, the top 1 percent of families owned 48 percent of the total financial wealth in the country. Of course, income inequality is less extreme than wealth inequality — yet the significant increase of both in the 1980s reveals the fundamental virtues and vices of unbridled capitalist markets. These markets yield *efficiency* and *ingenuity* in regard to what consumers desire and what products cost. At the same time they increase *inequality* and *isolation* in regard to what the most vulnerable people need and which basic social goods are available to them.

The major *economic* legacy of Reaganomics was to increase the disparity between rich and poor and to downsize the American middle class. Our social structure began to look less like a diamond and more like an hourglass. More hours of work were required to sustain a decent standard of living even as an undeniable decline in the quality of life set in — with increased crime, violence, disease (e.g., AIDS), tensions over race, gender and sexual orientation, decrepit public schools, ecological abuse and a faltering physical infrastructure. In short, Reaganomics resulted in waves of economic recovery, including millions of new jobs (many part-time), alongside a relative drop in the well-being of a majority of Americans.

Downward Mobility in the 1980s

During the 1970s, only a fifth of prime-age adults and their families suffered real income losses. In the decade ending in 1989, the proportion of those who lost income during their prime earning years jumped to a third, and half of that group experienced income losses exceeding 25%. About 42% of both blacks and high school dropouts saw their incomes shrink.

[Economist Stephen J.] Rose notes that those achieving very large income increases of more than 70% over 10 years lost ground, too. In the previous decade, some 35%, or more than a third of prime-age adults and their families, enjoyed such outsize real income gains. During the 1980s, the big winners fell to less than one in four.

Gene Koretz, *Business Week*, January 17, 1994.

The unintended *cultural* consequence of this economic legacy was a spiritual impoverishment in which the dominant conception of the good life consists of gaining access to power, pleasure and property, sometimes by any means. In other words, a fully crystallized market culture appeared in which civic institutions such as families, neighborhoods, unions, churches, synagogues, mosques held less and less sway, especially among young people. Is it a mere accident that nonmarket values like loyalty, commitment, service, care, concern — even tenderness — can hardly gain a secure foothold in such a market culture? Or that more and more of our children believe that life is a thoroughly hedonistic and narcissistic affair?

One of the telling moments of the '80s came when a member of the Federal Communications Commission boasted that when television was deregulated, "the marketplace will take care of children." And, to a significant degree, this unintentionally sad and sobering prophecy has come true. The entertainment industry, with its huge doses of sex and violence, has a disproportionate and often disgusting influence over us and our children. A creeping Zeitgeist of coldheartedness and mean-spiritedness accompanies this full-blown market culture. Everything revolves around buying and selling, promoting and advertising. This logic leads ultimately to the gangsterization of culture — the collapse of moral fabric and the shunning of personal responsibility in both vanilla suburbs and chocolate cities. Instead of reviving traditional values, the strong patriotism and social conservatism of the 1980s have ironically yielded a populace that is suspicious of the common good and addicted to narrow pleasures.

Culture Wars

The 1980s came to a close with the end of the cold war — yet the culture wars of a racially torn and market-driven American society loom large. A strategy of "positive polarization" (especially playing the racial card) has realigned the electorate into a predominantly white conservative Republican Party and a thoroughly bewildered centrist Democratic Party. This has helped produce a disgruntled citizenry that slouches toward cynicism, pessimism and even fatalism. Nearly half of all black children and 20 percent of all American children grow up in poverty, trapped in a cycle of despair and distrust.

The major paradox of the 1980s is that the decade ended with the collapse of moribund communist regimes of repression and regimentation — as well as the advent of more than 40 new social experiments in democracy around the world — just as American democracy is quietly threatened by internal decay. In other words, the far-reaching insights of Adam Smith's defense of the role of markets loom large in the eyes of former communist societies just as the cultural inanities of capitalism pointed out by Karl Marx become clearer in rich capitalist democracies — especially in the United States.

The market magic of the triumphant conservatism of the 1980s did help squeeze out fat and make American business more competitive in the brutal global economy. But we have yet to come to terms with the social costs. Confused citizens now oscillate between tragic resignation and vigorous attempts to hold at bay their feelings of impotence and powerlessness. Public life seems barren and vacuous. And gallant efforts to reconstruct public-mindedness in a Balkanized society of proliferating identities and constituencies seem farfetched, if not futile. Even the very art of public conversation — the precious activity of communicating with fellow citizens in a spirit of mutual respect and civility — appears to fade amid the noisy backdrop of name-calling and finger-pointing in flat sound bites.

Hope and Fear

The new decade of the 1990s begins with Americans hungry to make connections, to communicate their rage, anger, fury and hope. The new popularity of radio and TV talk shows is one symptom of this populist urge. Rap — the major form of popular music among young people — is another. The great American novel of the 1980s, the Nobel Prize laureate Toni Morrison's "Beloved," yearns to tell a "story not to be passed on" — a story of a great yet flawed American civilization afraid to confront its tragic past and fearful of its frightening future.

This fear now permeates much of America — fear of violent attack or vicious assault, fear of indecent exposure or malicious insult. Out of the '80s came a new kind of civic terrorism — physical and psychic — that haunts the public streets and private minds of America.

Race sits at the center of this terrifying moment. Although a small number of black men — who resemble myself or my son in appearance — commit a disproportionate number of violent crimes, the unfair stereotype of all black men as criminals persists. And despite the fact that most of these crimes are committed against black people, the national focus highlights primarily white victims.

Yet we all must assume our share of responsibility for the despair and degradation. The generational layers of social misery that afflict poor communities were rendered invisible in the 1980s not just by our government but by ourselves. Economic desperation coupled with social breakdown now threatens the very existence of impoverished communities in urban areas — with growing signs of the same forces at work in rural and suburban America. The drug and gun cultures among youth are the most visible symptoms of this nihilism. If we are to survive as a nation, the 1990s must be a decade in which candid and critical conversation takes place about race and poverty, rights and responsibilities, violence and despair.

The great comeback pop singer of the 1980s — Tina Turner — tragically croons, "What's Love Got to Do With It?" In a decade of glitz and greed, "who needs a heart when a heart can be broken?" And the most talented songwriting team in American popular music of the 1980s, Babyface and L. A. Reid, nod in their classic song, "My, My, My." Maybe in the '90s we can bring back some love, justice, humor and community.

KITSCH

Gilbert Highet (1906-78)

American classicist, born in Glasgow, Scotland. In 1951 Highet became a citizen of the United States. He was a professor of Greek and Latin at Columbia Univ. from 1938 to 1950 and a professor of Latin language and literature (1950-72). His writings include *The Classical Tradition* (1949); *The Art of Teaching* (1950); *Juvenal the Satirist* (1954); *Poets in a Landscape* (1957); *The Anatomy of Satire* (1962); *Vergil's Aeneid* (1972).

If you have ever passed an hour wandering through an antique shop (not looking for anything exactly, but simply looking), you must have noticed how your taste gradually grows numb, and then — if you stay — becomes perverted. You begin to see unsuspected charm in those hideous pictures of plump girls fondling pigeons, you develop a psychopathic desire for spinning wheels and cobblers' benches, you are apt to pay out good money for a bronze statuette of Otto von Bismarck, with a metal hand inside a metal frock coat and metal pouches under his metallic eyes. As soon as you take the things home, you realize that they are revolting. And yet they have a sort of horrible authority; you don't like them; you know how awful they are; but it is a tremendous effort to drop them in the garbage, where they belong.

To walk along a whole street of antique shops — that is an experience which shakes the very soul. Here is a window full of bulbous Chinese deities; here is another littered with Zulu assagais, Indian canoe paddles, and horse pistols which won't fire; the next shopfront is stuffed with gaudy Italian majolica vases, and the next, even worse, with Austrian pottery — tiny ladies and gentlemen sitting on lace cushions and wearing lace ruffles, with every frill, every wrinkle and reticulation translated into porcelain: pink; stiff; but fortunately not unbreakable. The nineteenth century produced an appalling amount of junky art like this, and sometimes I imagine that clandestine underground factories are continuing to pour it out like illicit drugs.

There is a name for such stuff in the trade, a word apparently of Russian origin, kitsch: it means vulgar showoff, and it is applied to anything that took a lot of trouble to make and is quite hideous.

It is paradoxical stuff, kitsch. It is obviously bad: so bad that you can scarcely understand how any human being would spend days and weeks making it, and how anybody else would buy it and take it home and keep it and dust it and leave it to her heirs. It is terribly ingenious, and terribly ugly, and utterly useless; and yet it has one of the qualities of good art — which is that, once seen, it is not easily forgotten. Of course it is found in all the arts: think of Milan Cathedral, or the statues in Westminster Abbey, or Liszt's settings of Schubert songs. There is a lot of it in the United States — for instance, the architecture of Miami, Florida, and Forest Lawn Cemetery in Los Angeles. Many of Hollywood's most ambitious historical films are superb kitsch. Most Tin Pan Alley love songs are perfect 100 per cent kitsch.

There is kitsch in the world of books also. I collect it. It is horrible, but I enjoy it.

The gem of my collection is the work of the Irish novelist Mrs. Amanda McKittrick Ros, whose masterpiece, *Delina Delaney*, was published about 1900. It is a stirringly romantic tale, telling how Delina, a fisherman's daughter from Erin Cottage, was beloved by Lord Gifford, the heir of Columbia Castle, and — after many trials and even imprisonment — married him. The story is dramatic, not to say impossible; but it is almost lost to view under the luxuriant style. Here, for example, is a sentence in which Mrs. Ros explains that her heroine used to earn extra cash by doing needlework.

> She tried hard to assist in keeping herself a stranger to her poor old father's slight income by the use of the finest production of steel, whose blunt edge eyed the reely covering with marked greed, and offered its sharp dart to faultless fabrics of flaxen fineness.

Revolting, but distinctive: what Mr. Polly called 'rockockyo' in manner. For the baroque vein, here is Lord Gifford saying goodby to his sweetheart:

> My darling virgin! my queen! my Delina! I am just in time to hear the toll of a parting bell strike its heavy weight of appalling softness against the weakest fibers of a heart of love, arousing and tickling its dormant action, thrusting the dart of evident separation deeper into its tubes of tenderness, and fanning the flame, already unextinguishable, into volumes of blaze.

Mrs. Ros had a remarkable command of rhetoric, and could coin an unforgettable phrase. She described her hero's black eyes as 'glittering jet revolvers.' When he became ill, she said he fell 'into a state of lofty fever' — doubtless because commoners have high fever, but lords have lofty fever. And her reflections on the moral degeneracy of society have rarely been equaled, in power and penetration:

> Days of humanity, whither hast thou fled? When bows of compulsion, smiles for the deceitful, handshakes for the dogmatic, and welcome for the tool of power live under your objectionable, unambitious beat, not daring to be checked by the tongue of candour because the selfish world refuses to dispense with her rotten policies. The legacy of your forefathers, which involved equity, charity, reason, and godliness, is beyond the reach of their frivolous, mushroom offspring — deceit, injustice, malice and unkindness — and is not likely to be codiciled with traits of harmony so long as these degrading vices of mock ambition fester the human heart.

Perhaps one reason I enjoy this stuff is because it so closely resembles a typical undergraduate translation of one of Cicero's finest perorations: sound and fury, signifying nothing. I regret only that I have never seen Mrs. Ros's poetry. One volume was called *Poems of Puncture* and another *Bayonets of Bastard Sheen*: alas, jewels now almost unprocurable. But at least I know the opening of her lyric written on first visiting St. Paul's Cathedral:

> Holy Moses, take a look,
> Brain and brawn in every nook!

Such genius is indestructible. Soon, soon now, some earnest researcher will be writing a Ph.D. thesis on Mrs. Amanda McKittrick Ros, and thus (as she herself might put it) conferring upon her dewy brow the laurels of concrete immortality.

Next to Mrs. Ros in my collection of kitsch is the work of the Scottish poet William McGonagall. This genius was born in 1830, but did not find his vocation until 1877. Poor and inadequate poets pullulate in every tongue, but (as the *Times Literary Supplement* observes) McGonagall 'is the only truly memorable bad poet in our language.' In his command of platitude and his disregard of melody, he was the true heir of William Wordsworth as a descriptive poet.

In one way his talents, or at least his aspirations, exceeded those of Wordsworth. He was at his best in describing events he had never witnessed, such as train disasters, shipwrecks, and sanguinary battles, and in picturing magnificent scenery he had never beheld except with the eye of the imagination. Here is his unforgettable Arctic landscape:

> Greenland's icy mountains are fascinating and grand,
> And wondrously created by the Almighty's command;
> And the works of the Almighty there's few can understand:
> Who knows but it might be a part of Fairyland?
>
> Because there are churches of ice, and houses glittering like glass,
> And for scenic grandeur there's nothing can it surpass,
> Besides there's monuments and spires, also ruins,
> Which serve for a safe retreat from the wild bruins.

> The icy mountains they're higher than a brig's topmast,
> And the stranger in amazement stands aghast
> As he beholds the water flowing off the melted ice
> Adown the mountain sides, that he cries out, Oh! how nice!

McGonagall also had a strong dramatic sense. He loved to tell of agonizing adventures, more drastic perhaps but not less moving than that related in Wordsworth's 'Vaudracour and Julia.' The happy ending of one of his 'Gothic' ballads is surely unforgettable:

> So thus ends the story of Hanchen, a heroine brave,
> That tried hard her master's gold to save,
> And for her bravery she got married to the miller's eldest son,
> And Hanchen on her marriage night cried Heaven's will be done.

These scanty selections do not do justice to McGonagall's ingenuity as a rhymester. His sound effects show unusual talent. Most poets would be baffled by the problem of producing rhymes for the proper names *General Graham* and *Osman Digna*, but McGonagall gets them into a single stanza, with dazzling effect:

> Ye sons of Great Britain, I think no shame
> To write in praise of brave General Graham!
> Whose name will be handed down to posterity without any stigma,
> Because, at the battle of El-Tab, he defeated Osman Digna.

One of McGonagall's most intense personal experiences was his visit to New York. Financially, it was not a success. In one of his vivid autobiographical sketches, he says, 'I tried occasionally to get an engagement from theatrical proprietors and music-hall proprietors, but alas! 'twas all in vain, for they all told me they didn't encourage rivalry.' However, he was deeply impressed by the architecture of Manhattan. In eloquent verses he expressed what many others have felt, although without adequate words to voice their emotion:

> Oh! Mighty City of New York, you are wonderful to behold,
> Your buildings are magnificent, the truth be it told;
> They were the only thing that seemed to arrest my eye,
> Because many of them are thirteen stories high.
>
> And the tops of the houses are all flat,
> And in the warm weather the people gather to chat;
> Besides on the house-tops they dry their clothes,
> And also many people all night on the house-tops repose.

Yet McGonagall felt himself a stranger in the United States. And here again his close kinship with Wordsworth appears. The Poet Laureate, in a powerful sonnet written at Calais, once reproached the English Channel for delaying his return by one of those too frequent storms in which (reckless tyrant!) it will indulge itself:

> Why cast ye back upon the Gallic shore,
> Ye furious waves! a patriotic Son
> Of England?

In the same vein McGonagall sings with rapture of his return to his 'ain countree':

And with regard to New York, and the sights I did see,
One street in Dundee is more worth to me,
And, believe me, the morning I sailed from New York,
For bonnie Dundee — my heart it felt as light as a cork.

Indeed, New York is a challenging subject for ambitious poets. Here, from the same shelf, is a delicious poem on the same theme, by Ezra Pound:

My City, my beloved
Thou art a maid with no breasts
Thou art slender as a silver reed.
Listen to me, attend me!
And I will breathe into thee a soul,
And thou shalt live for ever.

The essence of this kind of trash is incongruity. The kitsch writer is always sincere. He really means to say something important. He feels he has a lofty spiritual message to bring to an unawakened world, or else he has had a powerful experience which he must communicate to the public. But either his message turns out to be a majestic platitude, or else he chooses the wrong form in which to convey it — or, most delightful of all, there is a fundamental discrepancy between the writer and his subject, as when Ezra Pound, born in Idaho, addresses the largest city in the world as a maid with no breasts, and enjoins it to achieve inspiration and immortality by listening to him. This is like climbing Mount Everest in order to carve a head of Mickey Mouse in the east face.

Bad love poetry, bad religious poetry, bad mystical prose, bad novels both autobiographical and historical — one can form a superb collection of kitsch simply by reading with a lively and awakened eye. College songs bristle with it. The works of Father Divine are full of it — all the more delightful because in him it is usually incomprehensible. One of the Indian mystics, Sri Ramakrishna, charmed connoisseurs by describing the Indian scriptures (in a phrase which almost sets itself to kitsch-music) as

> fried in the butter of knowledge and steeped in the honey of love.

Bad funeral poetry is a rich mine of the stuff. Here, for example, is the opening of a jolly little lament, 'The Funeral' by Stephen Spender, apparently written during his pink period:

> Death is another milestone on their way,
> With laughter on their lips and with winds blowing round them
> They record simply
> How this one excelled all others in making driving belts.

Observe the change from humanism to communism. Spender simply took Browning's 'Grammarian's Funeral,' threw away the humor and the marching rhythm, and substituted wind and the Stakhanovist speed-up. Such also is a delicious couplet from Archibald MacLeish's elegy on the late Harry Crosby:

> He walks with Ernest in the streets in Saragossa
> They are drunk their mouths are hard they say *qué cosa.*

From an earlier romantic period, here is a splendid specimen.

Coleridge attempted to express the profound truth that men and animals are neighbors in a hard world; but he made the fundamental mistake of putting it into a monologue address to a donkey:

> Poor Ass! Thy master should have learnt to show
> Pity-best taught by fellowship of Woe!
> Innocent foal! thou poor despised forlorn!
> I hail thee brother. . . .

Once you get the taste for this kind of thing it is possible to find pleasure in hundreds of experiences which you might otherwise have thought either anesthetic or tedious: bad translations, abstract painting, grand opera . . . Dr. Johnson, with his strong sense of humor, had a fancy for kitsch, and used to repeat a poem in celebration of the marriage of the Duke of Leeds, composed by 'an inferiour domestick . . . in such homely rhymes as he could make':

> When the Duke of Leeds shall married be
> To a fine young lady of high quality,
> How happy will that gentlewoman be
> In his Grace of Leed's good company.
>
> She shall have all that's fine and fair,
> And the best of silk and sattin shall wear;
> And ride in a coach to take the air,
> And have a house in St. James's Square.

Folk poetry is full of such jewels. Here is the epitaph on an old gentleman from Vermont who died in a sawmill accident:

How shocking to the human mind
The log did him to powder grind.
God did command his soul away
His summings we must all obey.

Kitsch is well known in drama, although (except for motion pictures) it does not usually last long. One palmary instance was a play extolling the virtues of the Boy Scout movement, called *Young England.* It ran for a matter of years during the 1930's, to audiences almost wholly composed of kitsch-fanciers, who eventually came to know the text quite as well as the unfortunate actors. I can still remember the opening of one magnificent episode. Scene: a woodland glade. Enter the hero, a Scoutmaster, riding a bicycle, and followed by the youthful members of his troop. They pile bicycles in silence. Then the Scoutmaster raises his finger, and says (accompanied fortissimo by most of the members of the audience):

Fresh water must be our first consideration

In the decorative arts kitsch flourishes, and is particularly widespread in sculpture. One of my favorite pieces of bad art is a statue in Rockefeller Center, New York. It is supposed to represent Atlas, the Titan condemned to carry the sky on his shoulders. That is an ideal of somber, massive tragedy: greatness and suffering combined as in Hercules or Prometheus. But this version displays Atlas as a powerful moron, with a tiny little head, rather like the pan-fried young men who appear in the health magazines. Instead of supporting the heavens, he is lifting a spherical metal balloon: it is transparent, and quite empty; yet he is balancing insecurely on one foot like a furniture mover walking upstairs with a beach ball; and he is scowling like a mad baboon. If he ever gets the thing up, he will drop it; or else heave it onto a Fifth Avenue bus. It is a supremely ridiculous statue, and delights me every time I see it.

Perhaps you think this is a depraved taste. But really it is an extension of experience. At one end, Homer. At the other, Amanda McKittrick Ros. At one end, *Hamlet.* At the other, McGonagall, who is best praised in his own inimitable words:

> The poetry is moral and sublime
> And in my opinion nothing could be more fine.
> True genius there does shine so bright
> Like unto the stars of night.

Canadian Culture: A Brave New Spirit

Magaret Atwood

Born in 1939 in Ottawa, Ontario and educated at Victoria College, University of Toronto, Radcliffe College, Cambridge, Mass., and Harvard University. She taught at University of British Columbia, Sir George Williams University, University of Alberta, York University, Toronto. She was President of the Writers' Union of Canada from May, 1981 to May, 1982, and was President of International P.E.N., Canadian Centre (English Speaking) from 1984-1986.

What does Canada have to offer besides Wayne Gretsky, the "Great White North," the first downhill gold medal won by a North American, fantastic restaurants, and cities where you can go for a walk at night without getting disemboweled, where murder is so rare that it makes the front pages, where people actually use the "Keep Our Cities Clean" bins, and where you can get twenty extra cents on your dollar? In the cultural line, for instance? Quite a lot nowadays, but it's all quite recent. Being a Canadian used to be like having a big wart on the end of your nose. Not a handicap that would put you completely out of the running; more on the order of a socially embarrassing disfigurement that for the sake of everybody, including yourself, you should have removed.

This was especially true for artists. When I was growing up in the late 'fifties, "Canadian" and "artist" were mutually exclusive terms, and everyone knew that to be an actor or a writer or a painter you had to go to London or New York, like Donald Sutherland, Mordecai Richler, Christopher Plummer, Margaret Laurence, and anyone else for whom cheap English china and good places to ski weren't good enough. Toronto was the place you left on the weekends for a culturally enriching trip to Buffalo, N.Y. Theater was the Earle Gray Players, who put on Shakespeare in high school auditoriums, with students supplying the crowd scenes (for *Julius Caesar* you brought your own sheet). There was no ballet or opera. A writer did well to sell a hundred copies of a book of poetry and five hundred copies of a novel, and you were lucky if you got one review and a tea put on by a local women's group. When anyone said "Canadian culture," about the only thing that came to mind was "Hockey Night in Canada." That was Toronto, and the other cities were worse.

Why was it like that? It wasn't that Canadians were illiterate or uninterested in matters cultural. They read lots of English and American books, went to Hollywood and European movies in large numbers, flocked to imported plays and bought foreign paintings. Some blamed this state of affairs on size: Canada has an English-speaking population of a mere fourteen million or so, about the size of Australia's; and the French-speaking population is only slightly less than Sweden's. Some blamed it on the stifling Puritanism that made it impossible to import *Lady Chatterley's Lover* and divided "beer parlours" into Men Only and Ladies and Escorts sections. Some cited a deadening disease of the spirit known as "The Colonial Mentality": ex-colonies, such as New Zealand, Australia, and Canada, were doomed to see the great good place as being not where they were but back in the mystical motherland. Some noted the contempt for culture typical of frontier societies, the attitude that defined the arts as, at best, a frill and, at worst, pernicious and decadent. We still have that attitude; and at least once a year some member of Parliament causes a brief flurry by calling ballet a lot of creeps jumping around in long underwear, or asking why poets who use four-letter words should get grants. Some blamed it on the weather: how can you be creative, much less breathe, at fifty-below?

Despite these reasons, all of them true, all of them good, the whole picture changed suddenly in the mid-'sixties. Even Canadians — notoriously slow to recognize their own excellence, when they've managed to produce it — now realize that the country has undergone not a renaissance but a naissance over the past twenty years. Canadians still gobble up cultural imports at a great rate, just as they mainline international news and go through mountains of airplane tickets to foreign countries, but there's been an enormous shift.

In 1960, no one with any intellectual pretensions would have been caught reading a Canadian novel on the subway; this winter, Canadians held five of the ten slots on national bestseller lists. France has more than accepted Francophone writers such as Marie-

Clair Blais from Quebec and Antonine Maillet from New Brunswick. Northrop Frye and Marshall McLuhan are, to say the least, well-known.

Arthur Erickson, the architect, is in considerable demand. The excellence of the National Ballet and the Royal Winnipeg Ballet are taken for granted, and no one is too surprised when Karen Kain gets rave reviews in Moscow. Toronto alone has gone from no theater companies twenty-five years ago to a present total of over forty (in North America, second only to New York); it's currently renovating the spectacular Winter Garden Theatre, built in 1916 and unused for fifty years. Regional theaters are prospering from Newfoundland to British Columbia. Some of the plays they do are imports, but Canadian playwrights such as David Frenchy, Carol Bolt, James Reamay, and Rick Salutin are frequently performed as well. Toronto has fifteen or twenty dance companies ranging from tiny to huge.

Artists sell not only in their home towns but internationally (one thinks, for instance, of Riopelle, Jack Bush, and William Ronald). At a time when public galleries elsewhere are pulling in their horns, Ottawa is about to build a major national gallery to house its already extensive collection. Canadian studies programs are springing up all over the world, which is sometimes disconcerting to Canadians. We've been putting ourselves down for so long we can't quite believe it when places like France and Germany take us seriously.

Given the handicaps, why did this happen? It's a chicken-and-egg question: in this case, which came first, the excellence of the artists or audience appreciation and government support? I tend to think it was the artists, beginning with those in Quebec: but there's no doubt that the creation of the Canada Council, an arm's-length but government-funded arts granting agency, had a lot to do with the growth of the heavy money-swallowers, such as ballet companies, theater companies, and symphonies. The Council has also put money into publishing and has doled out grants to individual artists of every kind imaginable. For those who think such funding is only creeping socialism or smacks of ideological control, Canadians can only answer that, without it, we'd have to do without many of the arts.

This change was not without uproar. Canada, like any other country, has always been pulled two ways, inward and toward their own identity and the search for an indigenous art, outwards towards other countries and internationalism, sometimes called "internation standards." The United States has had its own episodes of conflict, notably in the 1840s, when the Anglophiles wanted American artists to do as the English did, and Young America was looking for a unique American genius. The results were Washington Irving for the Anglophiles and Melville for Young America, who didn't, however, find him American enough. The two categories are of course not mutually exclusive. International standards are appropriate for international forms, such as classical ballet and the Stratford Festival; but other kinds of creative artists work from a locally entered vision, as they do everywhere. Is Faulkner provincial because he wrote about Mississippi instead of spies in Venice? Canadians love travel, vicarious and otherwise; but they like to look in the mirror, too.

The problems of being a small cold toad in a large empty puddle with a large warm toad just south of you are nowhere more evident than in the film industry. Should you make films about being a small cold toad ("Canadian Content") or should you try to appeal to the large warm toad ("Commercial Viability")? Very early on there were Canadian films (*Nanook of the North* was one of ours), but Hollywood competition and the takeover of most of the distribution left Canadian filmmakers filling an otherwise unwanted ecological niche: short shorts. The National Film Board specialized in tiny perfect films, with experimental genius Norman McLaren as its recognized leading light.

In the past decade there's been a film renaissance predicted at least every three years, and films have indeed been made, propped up by various forms of legislation and tax write-off; but Canada has yet to catch up with Australia in the small-budget honest-and-charming-but-with-guts category. It has too often either tried to be Hollywood and failed, or turned to moneymakers about giant leeches coming out of your armpits or whores with hearts of bankable bullion. But there are signs of a breakthrough, yet again: Ralph Thomas' *Ticket to Heaven*, about a man who gets his head vacuumed by a religious cult, played to critical shrugs in Canada but around-the-block lines in the U.S.; Don Shebib's *Heartaches*, with Margot Kidder, is doing nicely; Giles Carles' *Les Plouffes* is impressing France.

For the States, Canada has at the moment something else to offer. These are tough times for artists everywhere; and even in the States, land of proverbial plenty, the pinch is being felt. All the money given to the arts by the U.S. Government is sufficient to run the Pentagon for eight hours, and that was last year. Artists in the States are understandably gloomy. Under these circumstances Canada may turn out to be a new kind of role model: how to make something from nothing, against enormous odds, and survive while doing it. For the 1980s, it's a good trick to know.

Columbus In Chains

Jamaica Kincaid

Award-winning novelist, short-story writer, and essayist who grew up on the West Indian island of Antigua. Her fiction includes *At the Bottom of the River, Annie John,* and *Lucy.* "Columbus in Chains," was originally published as a short story in the *New Yorker* and then became a chapter in *Annie John* (1985).

Outside, as usual, the sun shone, the trade winds blew; on her way to put some starched clothes on the line, my mother shooed some hens out of her garden; Miss Dewberry baked the buns, some of which my mother would buy for my father and me to eat with our afternoon tea; Miss Henry brought the milk, a glass of which I would drink with my lunch, and another glass of which I would drink with the bun from Miss Dewberry; my mother prepared our lunch; my father noted some perfectly idiotic thing his partner in housebuilding, Mr. Oatie, had done, so that over lunch he and my mother could have a good laugh.

The Anglican church bell struck eleven o'clock — one hour to go before lunch. I was then sitting at my desk in my classroom. We were having a history lesson — the last lesson of the morning. For taking first place over all the other girls, I had been given a prize, a copy of a book called *Roman Britain*, and I was made prefect of my class. What a mistake the prefect part had been, for I was among the worst-behaved in my class and did not at all believe in setting myself up as a good example, the way a prefect was supposed to do. Now I had to sit in the preface's seat — the first seat in the front row, the seat from which I could stand up and survey quite easily my classmates. From where I sat I could see out the window. Sometimes when I looked out, I could see the sexton going over to the minister's house. The sexton's daughter, Hilarene, a disgusting model of good behavior and keen attention to scholarship, sat next to me, since she took second place. The minister's daughter, Ruth, sat in the last row, the row reserved for all the dunce girls. Hilarene, of course, I could not stand. A girl that good would never do for me. I would probably not have cared so much for first place if I could be sure it would not go to her. Ruth I liked, because she was such a dunce and came from England and had yellow hair. When I first met her, I used to walk her home and sing bad songs to her just to see her turn pink, as if I had spilled hot water all over her.

Our books, *A History of the West Indies*, were open in front of us. Our day had begun with morning prayers, then a geometry lesson, then it was over to the science building for a lesson in "Introductory Physics" (not a subject we cared much for), taught by the most dingy-toothed Mr. Slacks, a teacher from Canada, then precious recess, and now this, our history lesson. Recess had the usual drama: this time, I coaxed Gwen out of her disappointment at not being allowed to join the junior choir. Her father — how many times had I wished he would become a leper and so be banished to a leper colony for the rest of my long and happy life with Gwen — had forbidden it, giving as his reason that she lived too far away from church, where choir rehearsals were conducted, and that it would be dangerous for her, a young girl, to walk home alone at night in the dark. Of course, all the streets had lamplight, but it was useless to point that out to him. Oh, how it would have pleased us to press and rub our knees together as we sat in our pew while pretending to pay dose attention to Mr. Simmons, our choirmaster, as he waved his baton up and down and across, and how it would have pleased us even more to walk home together, alone in the "early dusk" (the way Gwen had phrased it, a ready phrase always on her tongue), stopping, if there was a full moon, to lie down in a pasture and expose our bosoms in the moonlight. We had heard that full moonlight would make our breasts grow to a size we would like. Poor Gwen! When I first heard from her that she was one of ten children, right on the spot I told her that I would love only her, since her mother already had so many other people to love.

Our teacher, Miss Edward, paced up and down in front of the class in her usual way. In front of her desk stood a small table, and on it stood the dunce cap. The dunce cap was in the shape of a coronet, with an adjustable opening in the back, so that it could fit any head. It was made of cardboard with a shiny gold paper covering and the word "DUNCE" in shiny red paper on the front.

When the sun shone on it, the dunce cap was all aglitter, almost as if you were being tricked into thinking it a desirable thing to wear. As Miss Edward paced up and down, she would pass between us and the dunce cap like an eclipse. Each Friday morning, we were given a small test to see how well we had learned the things taught to us all week. The girl who scored lowest was made to wear the dunce cap all day the following Monday. On many Mondays, Ruth wore it — only, with her short yellow hair, when the dunce cap was sitting on her head she looked like a girl attending a birthday party in *The Schoolgirl's Own Annual.*

It was Miss Edward's way to ask one of us a question the answer to which she was sure the girl would not know and then put the same question to another girl who she was sure would know the answer. The girl who did not answer correctly would then have to repeat the correct answer in the exact words of the other girl. Many times, I had heard my exact words repeated over and over again, and I liked it especially when the girl doing the repeating was one I didn't care about very much. Pointing a finger at Ruth, Miss Edward asked a question the answer to which was "On the third of November 1493, a Sunday morning, Christopher Columbus discovered Dominica." Ruth, of course, did not know the answer, as she did not know the answer to many questions about the West Indies. I could hardly blame her. Ruth had come all the way from England. Perhaps she did not want to be in the West Indies at all. Perhaps she wanted to be in England, where no one would remind her constantly of the terrible things her ancestors had done; perhaps she had felt even worse when her father was a missionary in Africa. I could see how Ruth felt from looking at her face. Her ancestors had been the masters, while ours had been the slaves. She had such a lot to be ashamed of, and by being with us every day she was always being reminded. We could look everybody in the eye, for our ancestors had done nothing wrong except just sit somewhere, defenseless. Of course, sometimes, what with our teachers and our books, it was hard for us to tell on which side we really now belonged — with the masters or the slaves — for it was all history, it was all in the past, and everybody behaved differently now; all of us celebrated Queen Victoria's birthday, even though she had been dead a long time. But we, the descendants of the slaves, knew quite well what had really happened, and I was sure that if the tables had been turned we would have acted differently; I was sure that if our ancestors had gone from Africa to Europe and come upon the people living there, they would have taken a proper interest in the Europeans on first seeing them, and said, "How nice," and then gone home to tell their friends about it.

I was sitting at my desk, having these thoughts to myself. I don't know how long it had been since I lost track of what was going on around me. I had not noticed that the girl who was asked the question after Ruth failed — a girl named Hyacinth — had only got a part of the answer correct. I had not noticed that after these two attempts Miss Edward had launched into a harangue about what a worthless bunch we were compared to girls of the past. In fact, I was no longer on the same chapter we were studying. I was way ahead, at the end of the chapter about Columbus's third voyage. In this chapter, there was a picture of Columbus that took up a whole page, and it was in color — one of only five color pictures in the book. In this picture, Columbus was seated in the bottom of a ship. He was wearing the usual three-quarter trousers and a shirt with enormous sleeves, both the trousers and shirt made of maroon-colored velvet. His hat, which was cocked up on one side of his head, had a gold feather in it, and his black shoes had huge gold buckles. His hands and feet were bound up in chains, and he was sitting there staring off into space, looking quite dejected and miserable. The picture had as a title "Columbus in Chains," printed at the bottom of the page. What had happened was that the usually quarrelsome Columbus had got into a disagreement with people who were even more quarrelsome, and a man named Bobadilla, representing King Ferdinand and Queen Isabella, had sent him back to Spain fettered in chains attached to the bottom of a ship. What just desserts, I thought, for I did not like Columbus. How I loved this picture — to see the usually triumphant Columbus, brought so low, seated at the bottom of a boat just watching things go by. Shortly after I first discovered it in my history book, I heard my mother read out loud to my father a letter she had received from her sister, who still lived with her mother and father in the very same Dominica, which is where my mother came from. Ma Chess was fine, wrote my aunt, but Pa Chess was not well. Pa Chess was having a bit of trouble with his limbs; he was not able to go about as he pleased; often he had to depend on someone else to do one thing or another for him. My mother read the letter in quite a state, her voice rising to a higher pitch with each sentence. After she read the part about Pa Chess's stiff limbs, she turned to my father and laughed as she said, "So the great man can no longer just get up and go. How I would love to see his face now!" When I next saw the picture of Columbus sitting there all locked up in his chains, I wrote under it the words "The Great Man Can No Longer Just Get Up and Go." I had written this out with my fountain pen, and in Old English lettering — a script I had recently mastered. As I sat there looking at the picture, I traced the words with my pen over and over, so that the letters grew big and you could read what I had written from not very far away. I don't know how long it was before I heard that my name, Annie John, was being said by this bellowing dragon in the form of Miss Edward bearing down on me.

I had never been a favorite of hers. Her favorite was Hilarene. It must have pained Miss Edward that I so often beat out Hilarene. Not that I liked Miss Edward and wanted her to like me back, but as the other teachers regarded me with much affection, would always tell my mother that I was the most charming student they had ever had, beamed at me when they saw me coming, and were very sorry when they had to write some version of this on my report card: "Annie is an unusually bright girl. She is well behaved in class, at least in the presence of her masters and mistresses, but behind their backs and outside the classroom quite the opposite is true." When my mother read this or something like it, she would burst into tears. She had hoped to display, with a great flourish, my report card to her friends, along with whatever prize I had won. Instead, the report card would have to take a place at the bottom of the old trunk in which she kept any important thing that had to do with me. I became not a favorite of Miss Edward's in the following way: Each Friday afternoon, the girls in the lower forms were given, instead of a last lesson period, an extra-long recess. We were to use this in lady-like recreation — walks, chats about the novels and poems we were reading, showing each other the new embroidery stitches we had learned to master in home class, or something just as seemly. Instead, some of the girls would play a game of cricket or rounders or stones, but most of us would go to the far end of the school grounds and play band. In this game, of which teachers and parents disapproved and which was sometimes absolutely forbidden, we would place our arms around each other's waist or shoulders, forming lines of ten or so girls, and then we would dance from one end of the school grounds to the other. As we danced, we would sometimes chat these words: "Tee la la la, come go. Tee la la la, come go." At other times we would sing a popular calypso song which usually had lots of unladylike words to it. Up and down the schoolyard, away from our teachers, we would dance and sing. At the end of recess — forty-five minutes — we were missing ribbons and other ornaments from our hair, the pleats of our linen tunics became unset, the collars of our blouses were pulled out, and we were soaking wet all the way down to our bloomers. When the school bell rang, we would make a whooping sound, as if in a great panic, and then we would throw ourselves on top of each other as we laughed and shrieked. We would then run back to our classes, where we prepared to file into the auditorium for evening prayers. After that, it was home for the weekend. But how could we go straight home after all that excitement? No sooner were we on the street than we would form little groups, depending on the direction we were headed in. I was never keen on joining them on the way home, because I was sure I would run into my mother. Instead my friends and I would go to our usual place near the back of the churchyard and sit on the tombstones of people who had been buried there way before slavery was abolished, in 1833. We would sit and sing bad songs, use forbidden words, and, of course, show each other various parts of our bodies. While some of us watched, the others would walk up and down on the large tombstones showing off their legs. It was immediately a popular idea; everybody soon wanted to do it. It wasn't long before many girls — the ones whose mothers didn't pay strict attention to what they were doing — started to come to school on Fridays wearing not bloomers under their uniforms but underpants trimmed with lace and satin frills. It also wasn't long before an end came to all that. One Friday afternoon, Miss Edward, on her way home from school, took a shortcut through the churchyard. She must have heard the commotion we were making, because there she suddenly was, saying, "What is the meaning of this?" — just the very thing someone like her would say if she came unexpectedly on something like us. It was obvious that I was the ringleader. Oh, how I wished the ground would open up and take her in, but it did not. We all, shamefacedly, slunk home, I with Miss Edward at my side. Tears came to my mother's eyes when she heard what I had done. It was apparently such a bad thing that my mother couldn't bring herself to repeat my misdeed to my father in my presence. I got the usual punishment of dinner alone, outside under the breadfruit tree, but added on to that, I was not allowed to go to the library on Saturday, and on Sunday, after Sunday school and dinner, I was not allowed to take a stroll in the botanical gardens, where Gwen was waiting for me in the bamboo grove.

That happened when I was in the first form. Now here Miss Edward stood. Her whole face was on fire. Her eyes were bulging out of her head. I was sure that at any minute they would land at my feet and roll away. The small pimples on her face, already looking as if they were constantly irritated, now ballooned into huge, on-the-verge-of-exploding boils. Her head shook from side to side. Her strange bottom, which she carried high in the air, seemed to rise up so high that it almost touched the ceiling. Why did I not pay attention, she said. My impertinence was beyond endurance. She then found a hundred words for the different forms my impertinence took. On she went. I was just getting used to this amazing bellowing when suddenly she was speechless. In fact, everything stopped. Her eyes stopped, her bottom stopped, her pimples stopped. Yes she had got close enough so that her eyes caught a glimpse of what I had done to my textbook. The glimpse soon led to closer inspection. It was bad enough that I had defaced my schoolbook by writing in it. That I should write under the picture of Columbus "The Great Man. . . " etc. was just too much. I had gone too far this time, defaming one of the great men in history, Christopher Columbus, discoverer of the island that was my home. And now look at me. I was not even hanging my head in remorse. Had my peers ever seen anyone so arrogant, so blasphemous?

I was sent to the headmistress, Miss Moore. As punishment, I was removed from my position as prefect, and my place was taken by the odious Hilarene. As an added punishment, I was ordered to copy Books I and II of *Paradise Lost*, by John Milton, and to have it done a week from that day. I then couldn't wait to get home to lunch and the comfort of my mother's kisses and arms. I had nothing to worry about there yet; it would be a while before my mother and father heard of my bad deeds. What a terrible morning! Seeing my mother would be such a tonic — something to pick me up.

When I got home, my mother kissed me absentmindedly. My father had got home ahead of me, and they were already deep in conversation, my father regaling her with some unusually outlandish thing the oaf Mr. Oatie had done. I washed my hands and took my place at table. My mother brought me my lunch. I took one smell of it, and I could tell that it was the much hated breadfruit. My mother said not at all, it was a new kind of rice imported from Belgium, and not breadfruit, mashed and forced through a ricer, as

I thought. She went back to talking to my father. My father could hardly get a few words out of his mouth before she was a jelly-fish of laughter. I sat there, putting my food in my mouth. I could not believe that she couldn't see how miserable I was and so reach out a hand to comfort me and caress my cheek, the way she usually did when she sensed that something was amiss with me. I could not believe how she laughed at everything he said, and how bitter it made me feel to see how much she liked him. I ate my meal. The more I ate of it, the more I was sure that it was breadfruit. When I finished, my mother got up to remove my plate. As she started out the door, I said, "Tell me, really, the name of the thing I just ate."

My mother said, "You just ate some breadfruit. I made it look like rice so that you would eat it. It's very good for you, filled with lots of vitamins." As she said this, she laughed. She was standing half inside the door, half outside. Her body was in the shade of our house, but her head was in the sun. When she laughed, her mouth opened to show off big, shiny, sharp white teeth. It was as if my mother had suddenly turned into a crocodile.

Section III : Society, Politics and Science

Bill Gates' New Rules

William Bill H. Gates (1955-)

Chairman and chief software architect of Microsoft Corporation, the worldwide leader in software, services and Internet technologies for personal and business computing. Wrote *Business @ the Speed of Thought* (1999), a book that shows how computer technology can solve business problems in fundamentally new ways.

If the 1980s were about quality and the 1990s were about re-engineering, then the 2000s will be about velocity. About how quickly business itself will be transacted. About how information access will alter the lifestyle of consumers and their expectations of business. Quality improvements and business-process improvements will occur far faster. When the increase in velocity is great enough, the very nature of business changes.

To function in the digital age, we have developed a new digital infrastructure. It's like the human nervous system. Companies need to have that same kind of nervous system — the ability to run smoothly and efficiently, to respond quickly to emergencies and opportunities, to quickly get valuable information to the people in the company who need it, the ability to quickly make decisions and interact with customers.

The successful companies of the next decade will be the ones that use digital tools to reinvent the way they work. To make digital information flow an intrinsic part of your company, here are 12 key steps.

1. INSIST THAT COMMUNICATION FLOW THROUGH E-MAIL

For a large company to be able to maneuver as well as or better than a smaller competitor is a testament to both the energy of the employees and the use of digital systems. Personal initiative and responsibility are enhanced in an environment that fosters discussion. E-mail, a key component of our digital nervous system, does just that. It helps turn middle managers from information filleters into "doers." There's no doubt that e-mail flattens the hierarchical structure of an organization. It encourages people to speak up. It encourages managers to listen. That's why, when customers ask what's the first thing they can do to get more value out of their information systems and foster collaboration in their companies, I always answer, "E-mail."

I read all the e-mail that employees send me, and I pass items on to people for action. I find unsolicited mail an incredibly good way to stay aware of the attitudes and issues affecting the many people who work at Microsoft. The old saying "Knowledge is power" sometimes makes people hoard knowledge. They believe that knowledge hoarding makes them indispensable. Power comes not from knowledge kept but from knowledge shared. A company's values and reward system should reflect that idea.

I like good news as much as the next person, but it also puts me in a skeptical frame of mind. I wonder what bad news I'm not hearing. When somebody sends me an e-mail about an account we've won, I always think, "There are a lot of accounts nobody has sent mail about. Does that mean we've lost all of those?" A good e-mail system ensures that bad news can travel fast, but your people have to be willing to send you the news. You have to be consistently receptive to bad news, and then you have to act on it. Sometimes I think my most important job as CEO is to listen for bad news. If you don't act on it, your people will eventually stop bringing bad news to your attention. And that's the beginning of the end.

2. STUDY SALES DATA ONLINE TO SHARE INSIGHTS EASILY

"Know your numbers" is a fundamental precept of business. You need to gather your business's data at every step of the way and in every interaction with your customers. With your partners too. Then you need to understand what the data means.

Making data digital from the start can trigger a whole range of positive events. The Coca-Cola Co. is collecting data directly from smart vending machines via cellular phones or infrared signals. A PC-based restocking program at the local bottler office analyzes the data and produces a delivery slip that tells drivers which products and locations need to get stocked the next day.

Taking advantage of digital data at the source can even create new business opportunities. A pilot program in Texas lets customers use a credit or debit card to pay for Coke drinks while fueling at a gas station. Since most people who pay at the pump don't go into the building, the digital sales system at the pump creates a whole segment of new customers for Coke.

When figures are in electronic form, knowledge workers can study them, annotate them, look at them in any amount of detail or in any view they want and pass them around for collaboration. Going digital changes your business.

3. SHIFT KNOWLEDGE WORKERS INTO HIGH-LEVEL THINKING

A company's middle managers and line employees, not just its high-level executives, need to see business data. They're the people who need precise, actionable data because they're the ones who need to act. They need an immediate, constant flow and rich views of the right information. Companies should spend less time protecting financial data from employees and more time teaching them to analyze and act on it.

At McDonald's, until recently, sales data had to be manually "touched" several times before making its way to the people who needed it. Today McDonald's is well on the way to installing a

new information system that uses PCs and Web technologies to tally sales at all its restaurants in real time. As soon as you order two Happy Meals, a McDonald's marketing manager will know. Rather than superficial or anecdotal data, the marketer will have hard, factual data for tracking trends. What I'm describing here is a new level of information analysis that enables knowledge workers to turn passive data into active information — what M.I.T.'s Michael Dertouzos calls information-as-a-verb.

4. USE DIGITAL TOOLS TO CREATE VIRTUAL TEAMS

A collaborative culture, reinforced by information flow, makes it possible for smart people all over a company to be in touch with each other. When you get a critical mass of high-IQ people working in concert, the energy level shoots way up. Knowledge management is a fancy term for a simple idea. You're managing data, documents and people's efforts. Your aim should be to enhance the way people work together, share ideas, sometimes wrangle and build on one another's ideas — and then act in concert for a common purpose.

Jacques (Jac) Nasser, president and CEO of Ford, sends e-mail to Ford employees worldwide, sharing news — the good and the bad — with everybody. No one screens the e-mail. He talks straight to the employees. He also reads hundreds of responses he gets each month and assigns a member of his team to reply to any that need follow-up.

Getting people motivated to take on responsibility is not a question of organizational structure so much as organizational attitude. Digital tools are the best way to open the door and add flexibility. If the right people can be working on the issues within hours instead of days, a business obtains a huge advantage.

5. CONVERT EVERY PAPER PROCESS TO A DIGITAL PROCESS

In 1996 I decided to look into the ways that Microsoft, a big advocate of replacing paper with electronic forms, was still using paper. To my surprise, we had printed 350,000 paper copies of sales reports that year. I asked for a copy of every paper form we used. The thick binder that landed on my desk contained hundreds and hundreds of forms.

Paper consumption was only a symptom of a bigger problem, though: administrative processes that were too complicated and time-intensive. Using our intranet to replace paper forms has produced striking results for us. We have reduced the number of paper forms from more than 1,000 to a company-wide total of 60 forms.

Companies talk about rewarding initiative and keeping workers focused on business. When employees see a company eliminate bottlenecks and time-draining routine administrative chores from their workdays, they know the company values their time — and wants them to use it profitably.

6. USE DIGITAL TOOLS TO ELIMINATE SINGLE-TASK JOBS

An acquaintance of mine had an uncle who spent 25 years at an auto plant in Flint, Mich., tacking chrome strips and other finish parts onto automobiles. It was a good job in the years immediately after World War II, but it followed the classic Industrial Age approach: break a process into small, discrete tasks and assign each to one person who does it over and over "the one best way."

In the new organization, the worker is no longer a cog in the machine but is an intelligent part of the overall process. Having people focus on whole processes allows them to tackle more interesting, challenging work. A one-dimensional job (a task) can be eliminated, automated or rolled into a bigger process.

General Motors launched the Saturn Corp. back in 1985 to create not only a brand-new car from scratch but a brand-new way of building cars and empowering workers. Teams are tight, autonomous units. Each team has a specific function, such as building engines or doors, and each team member is trained to do approximately 30 different jobs in that area, so that people don't get stale from doing repetitive tasks.

Through a Web interface, the worker can retrieve data from a database, automatically load the data into a spreadsheet and pivot through the data to analyze it by part and type of problem. Give your workers more sophisticated jobs along with better tools, and you'll discover that your employees will become more responsible and bring more intelligence to their work.

One-dimensional, repetitive work is exactly what computers, robots and other machines are best at — and what human workers are poorly suited to and almost uniformly despise. In the digital age, you need to make knowledge workers out of every employee possible.

7. CREATE A DIGITAL FEEDBACK LOOP

Since Michael Hammer and James Champy introduced the concept of reengineering in 1993, companies the world over have been re-examining their business processes. When I read their book, *Reengineering the Corporation*, three of their ideas really stood out for me. The first is that you need to step back periodically to take a hard look at your processes. Do they solve the right problems? Can they be simplified? The second is that if you cut a job into too many pieces and involve too many people, nobody can see the whole process and the work will bog down. The third, closely related to the second, is that too many hand-offs create too many likely points of failure.

Creating a new process is a major project. You should have a specific definition of success, a specific beginning and end in terms of time and tasks, intermediate milestones and a budget. The best projects are those in which people have the customer scenario clearly in mind. That's true of process projects too.

Digital technology makes it possible to develop much better

processes instead of being stuck with variations on the old paper processes that give you only incremental improvements. You need to be flexible in the face of evolving requirements. You should have a crisp decision process to evaluate change, including a provision for re-evaluating your original project goals.

8. USE DIGITAL SYSTEMS TO ROUTE CUSTOMER COMPLAINTS IMMEDIATELY

Listening to customers means hearing their complaints about current product shortcomings. But getting bad news from customers passed all the way to the product design groups is surprisingly hard to do.

I recommend the following approach:

1. Focus on your most unhappy customers.
2. Use technology to gather rich information on their unhappy experiences with your product and to find out what they want you to put into the product.
3. Use technology to drive the news to the right people in a hurry.

If you do these three things, you'll turn those draining bad news experiences into an exhilarating process of improving your product or service. Unhappy customers are always a concern. They're also your greatest opportunity. Companies that invest early in digital nervous systems to capture, analyze and capitalize on customer input will differentiate themselves from competition. You should examine customer complaints more often than company financials. And your digital systems should help you convert bad news to improved products and services.

9. USE DIGITAL COMMUNICATION TO REDEFINE THE BOUNDARIES

The internet allows a company to focus far more than in the past by changing which employees work within the walls and which work outside in an adjunct, consulting or partnering role.

For Microsoft, outsourcing has been a way to temper the expansion of our work force and reduce management overhead, but it hasn't stopped the growth of our work force. The Web work style, in which each contributor or company organizes itself optimally, enables us to extend our electronic web of partnerships and — I hope — keeps us from growing big in the wrong areas and becoming ineffective through too much overhead.

As a business manager, you need to take a hard look at your core competencies. Revisit the areas of your company that aren't directly involved in those competencies, and consider whether Web technologies can enable you to spin off those tasks. Let another company take over the management responsibilities for that work, and use modern communications technology to work closely with the people — now partners instead of employees — doing the work. In the Web work style, employees can push the freedom the Web provides to its limits.

10. TRANSFORM EVERY BUSINESS PROCESS INTO JUST-IN-TIME DELIVERY

M.I.T.'s Nicholas Negroponte describes the difference between physical products and information products in the digital age as the difference between moving atoms around (physical products such as cars and computers) and moving bits around (electronic products such as financial analyses and news broadcasts). Producers of bits can use the Internet to reduce their delivery times to practically zero. Producers of atoms still can't beam the physical objects through space, but they can use bitspeed — digital coordination of all kinds — to bring reaction time down dramatically.

In some industries, the issue is not so much faster time to market as it is maintaining time to market in the face of astronomically rising complexity. Intel, for instance, has consistently had a 90-day production cycle for its chips, which power most PCs. Intel expects to maintain this 90-day production rate despite the increasing complexity of the microprocessor.

Ultimately the most important "speed" issue for companies is cultural. It's changing the perceptions within a company about the rapidity with which everybody has to move. Everybody must realize that if you don't meet customer demand quickly enough, without sacrificing quality, a competitor will.

11. USE DIGITAL DELIVERY TO ELIMINATE THE MIDDLE MAN

In 1995, in *The Road Ahead,* I used the term friction-free capitalism to describe how the Internet was helping to create Adam Smith's ideal marketplace, in which buyers and sellers can easily find one another without taking much time or spending much money.

If you're a middleman, the Internet's promise of cheaper prices and faster service can "disintermediate" you, eliminate your role of assisting the transaction between the producer and the consumer. If the Internet is about to disintermediate you, one tack is to use the Internet to get back into the action.

That's what Egghead.com (formerly Egghead), a major retail software chain, did after struggling for several years. Egghead closed all of its physical stores nationwide in 1998 and set up shop exclusively on the Internet. Egghead now offers a number of new online programs that take advantage of the Internet, such as electronic auctions for about 50 different categories of hardware and software and for reconditioned computers. It puts special liquidation prices on systems available on its website and sends out a weekly e-mail "Hot List" with exclusive offers available only to e-mail subscribers.

For the majority of products, which are available through many outlets, consumers will be the greatest beneficiaries. For unique products and services, sellers will find more potential customers and may command higher prices. The more consumers adopt the Web life-style, the closer the economy will move toward Adam Smith's perfect market in all areas of commerce.

12. USE DIGITAL TOOLS TO HELP CUSTOMERS SOLVE PROBLEMS FOR THEMSELVES

As electronic commerce booms, it's not just the middlemen who will find creative ways to use the Internet to strengthen their relationships and customers. The merchants who treat e-commerce as more than a digital cash register will do the best.

Dell was one of the first major companies to move to e-commerce. A global computer supplier with more than $18 billion in revenue, Dell began selling its products online in mid-1996. The company's online business quickly rose from $1 million a week to $1 million a day. Soon it jumped to $3 million a day, then $5 million. It's now risen to $14 million.

Michael Dell characterizes the business today as "different combinations of face-to-face, ear-to-ear and keyboard-to-keyboard. Each has its place. The Internet doesn't replace people. It makes them more efficient. By moving routine interactions to the Web and enabling customers to do some things for themselves, we've freed up our salespeople to do more meaningful things with customers."

Smart companies will combine Internet services and personal contact in programs that give their customers the benefits of both kinds of interaction. You want to move pure transactions to the

Internet, use online communication for information sharing and routine communication, and reserve face-to-face interaction for the activities that add the most value.

As I said in *The Road Ahead*, we always overestimate the change that will occur in the next two years and underestimate the change that will occur in the next 10. Don't let yourself be lulled into inaction.

You know you have built an excellent digital nervous system when information flows through your organization as quickly and naturally as thought in a human being and when you can use technology to marshal and coordinate teams of people as quickly as you can focus an individual on an issue. It's business at the speed of thought. END.

Of Corn and Butterflies

Frederic Golden

Time magazine writer

U.S. farmers are planting 20 million acres of bioengineered corn. Will it poison the monarchs?

With its flamboyant orange-and-black wings and incredible 1,000-mile migratory flights, the monarch butterfly is one of the world's best-known and most beloved insects. And like a miner's canary, it has become a kind of biological early-warning system, succumbing to environmental changes long before humans notice them. Last week the monarch sounded another alert — fanning new fears about bioengineered crops.

In a study published in Nature, Cornell entomologist John Losey and his colleagues reported that pollen from corn made pest-resistant by the addition of bacterial genes could spell trouble for monarchs. In his experiments, Losey scattered pollen from the genetically modified corn onto milkweed — the butterfly's only food during its larval or caterpillar stage — and watched what happened with alarm. Most of the caterpillars that ate these leaves either died or were stunted.

The Cornell tests set off a flutter of concern not only for the survival of the monarchs — already threatened by logging in their winter roosts in the mountains west of Mexico City and by pesticides in their Cornbelt breeding grounds — but also over our increasing dependence on high-tech, genetically engineered food crops. “This is a heads-up,” warns entomologist Fred Gould of North Carolina state University.

Approved by the environmental Protection Agency in 1996, so-called Bt corn has become enormously popular with farmers, and now accounts for up to 25% of the U.S. corn crop, or about 20 million acres. by splicing DNA from the common soil bacterium Bacillus thuringiensis into the corn’s genes, scientists have created a plant that turns out the same toxin as the bug. While the toxin is deadly to the corn borer, which costs U.S. growers more than $1 billion annually, it is harmless to humans — as well as to such beneficial insects as ladybugs and honeybees. Indeed, organic farmers have long used Bt sprays as a natural pesticide.

With hundreds of millions of dollars at stake, agritech companies aren’t eager to draw sweeping conclusions from the Cornell experiments. “Obviously the work is preliminary and inconclusive,” says Monsanto spokesman Randy Krotz, minimizing the possibility that corn pollen could ever be blown far enough to affect monarch habitats. But it was just such a discovery — of pollen-dusted milkweed 200 ft. from the edge of cornfields — that prompted Losey’s study in the first place. Says he: “We asked ourselves,

'What would happen if the milkweed would be dusted with Bt [corn pollen]?'" His experiments quickly gave an answer: within four days, 44% of monarch larvae placed on the dusted leaves were dead, while controls survived unscathed.

Losey is eager to take the experiments into the field, to measure pollen density at various distances from its source so as to determine risk to monarch larvae at each site. Says Losey: "We have to weigh the costs and benefits [of Bt corn], then decide as a society what we want." But that decision may already have been made. The Bt gene is now regularly spliced into potatoes (as protection against the Colorado potato beetle) and cotton (against the boll weevil).

Five years after U.S. regulators approved the first genetically altered food crop, the "FlavrSavr" tomato, there are all manner of brave new foods on the way: beans and grains with more protein, caffeine-less coffee beans, strawberries packed with more natural sugars, and potatoes that soak up less fat during frying. At last count, says plant ecologist Allison Snow of Ohio State University, field trials have been conducted for some 50 gene-spliced food plants, including squash, melons, carrots, onions, peppers, apples and papayas.

But such tinkering can go awry. As even their proponents concede, spliced genes, like any other genes, can be picked up by wild species. The fear is that they will create what geneticist Norm Ellstrand of the University of California at Riverside, calls "a weedier weed" — a species, such as the superweed that turned up in France when sugar beets crossed accidentally with a wild relative, that is both harder to control and more ecologically disruptive. Scientists also fear that as use of Bt crops increases, so will resistance in the very pests they're aimed at, depriving organic farmers of a natural pesticide they'd come to trust.

Measures are being considered to avert such calamities — for example, ringing cornfields with patches of plain, old-fashioned corn so that not all pests become resistant. But these efforts haven't silenced critics, expecially in Britain, where a noisy debate is raging over what the London tabloids like to call "Frankenstein foods." Last week the British Medical Association called for a moratorium on commercial planting of all transgenic crops until scientists agree on their safety. In India, Monsanto is running into a p.r. buzz saw in its efforts to introduce a Bt cotton called Bollgard — even as it wrestles with continuing protests over its stalled plans to include in its new crops so-called terminator technology that would compel farmers to buy fresh seed for each planting.

Viewing the new crops as useful alternatives to pesticides, most scientists want work on them to continue, if more cautiously. The message from the monarchs, meanwhile, is that even the most well-intentioned biotechnologies are not risk-free.

THE NUCLEAR WINTER

Carl Edward Sagan **(1934-1996)**

Planetary scientists played a leading role in the Mariner, Viking, and Voyager spacecraft expeditions to the planets. made seminal contributions to the study of planetary atmospheres, planetary surfaces, the history of the Earth, and exobiology (the study of possible alien biochemistry and life forms). Books: *Cosmos* (science book), Contact (novel).

Into the eternal darkness, into fire, into ice.

Dante,
The Inferno

Except for fools and madmen, everyone knows that nuclear war would be an unprecedented human catastrophe. A more or less typical strategic warhead has a yield of 2 megatons, the explosive equivalent of 2 million tons of TNT. But 2 million tons of TNT is about the same as all the bombs exploded in World War II — a single bomb with the explosive power of the entire Second World War but compressed into a few seconds of time and an area 30 or 40 miles across . . .

In a 2-megaton explosion over a fairly large city, buildings would be vaporized, people reduced to atoms and shadows, outlying structures blown down like matchsticks and raging fires ignited. And if the bomb were exploded on the ground, an enormous crater, like those that can be seen through a telescope on the surface of the Moon, would be all that remained where midtown once had been. There are now more than 50,000 nuclear weapons, more than 13,000 megatons of yield, deployed in the arsenals of the United States and the Soviet Union — enough to obliterate a million Hiroshimas.

But there are fewer than 3000 cities on the Earth with populations of 100,000 or more. You cannot find anything like a million Hiroshima to obliterate. Prime military and industrial targets that are far from cities are comparatively rare. Thus, there are vastly more nuclear weapons than are needed for any plausible deterrence of a potential adversary.

Nobody knows, of course, how many megatons would be exploded in a real nuclear war. There are some who think that a nuclear war can be "contained", bottled up before it runs away to involve many of the world's arsenals. But a number of detailed analyses, war games run by the U.S. Department of Defense and official Soviet pronouncements, all indicate that this containment may be too much to hope for: Once the bombs begin exploding, communications failures, disorganization, fear, the necessity of making in minutes decisions affecting the fates of millions and the immense psychological burden of knowing that your own loved ones may already have been destroyed are likely to result in a nuclear paroxysm. Many investigators, including a number of studies for the U.S. government, envision the explosion of 5000 to 10,000 megatons — the detonation of tens of thousands of nuclear weapons that now sit quietly, inconspicuously, in missile silos, submarines and long-range bombers, faithful servants awaiting order.

The World Health Organization, in a recent detailed study chaired by Sune K. Bergstrom (the 1982 Nobel laureate in physiology and medicine), concludes that 1.1 billion people would be killed outright in such a nuclear war, mainly in the United States, the Soviet Union, Europe, China and Japan. An additional 1.1 billion people would suffer serious injuries and radiation sickness, for which medical help would be unavailable. It thus seems possible that more than 2 billion people — almost half of all the humans on Earth — would be destroyed in the immediate aftermath of a global thermonuclear war. This would represent by far the greatest disaster in the history of the human species and, with no other adverse effects, would probably be enough to reduce at least the Northern Hemisphere to a state of prolonged agony and barbarism. Unfortunately, the real situation would be much worse.

In technical studies of the consequences of nuclear weapons explosions, there has been a dangerous tendency to underestimate the results. This is partly due to a tradition of conservatism which generally works well in science but which is of more dubious applicability when the lives of billions of people are at stake. In the Bravo test of March 1, 1954, a 15-megaton thermonuclear bomb was exploded on Bikini Atoll. It had about double the yield expected, and there was an unanticipated last-minute shift in the wind direction. As a result, deadly radioactive fallout came down on Rongelap in the Marshall Islands, more than 200 kilometers away. Almost all the children on Rongelap subsequently developed thyroid nodules and lesions, and other longterm medical problems, due to the radioactive fallout.

Likewise, in 1973, it was discovered that high-yield airbursts will chemically burn the nitrogen in the upper air, converting it into oxides of nitrogen; these, in turn, combine with and destroy the protective ozone in the Earth's stratosphere. The surface of the Earth is shielded from deadly solar ultraviolet radiation by a layer of ozone so tenuous that, were it brought down to sea level, it would be only 3 millimeters thick. Partial destruction of this ozone layer can have serious consequences for the biology of the entire planet.

These discoveries, and others like them, were made by chance. They were largely unexpected. And now another consequence — by far the most dire — has been uncovered, again more or less by accident.

The U.S. Mariner 9 spacecraft, the first vehicle to orbit another planet, arrived at Mars in late 1971. The planet was enveloped in a global dust storm. As the fine particles slowly fell out, we were able to measure temperature changes in the atmosphere and on the surface. Soon it became clear what had happened:

The dust, lofted by high wind off the desert into the upper Martian atmosphere had absorbed the incoming sunlight and prevented much of it from reaching the ground. Heated by the sunlight, the dust warmed the adjacent air. But the surface, enveloped in partial darkness, became much chillier than usual Months later, after the dust fell out of the atmosphere, the upper air cooled and the surface warmed, both returning to their normal conditions. We were able to calculate accurately, from how much dust there was in the atmosphere, how cool the Martian surface ought to have been.

Afterwards, I and my colleagues, James B. Pollack and Brian Toon of NASA's Ames Research Center, were eager to apply these insights to the Earth. In a volcanic explosion, dust, aerosols are lofted into the high atmosphere. We calculated by how much the Earth's global temperature should decline after a major volcanic explosion and found that our results (generally a fraction of a degree) were in good accord with actual measurement. Joining forces with Richard Turco, who has studied the effects of nuclear weapons for many years, we then began to turn our attention to the climatic effects of nuclear war. [The scientific paper, "Global Atmospheric Consequences of Nuclear War," is written by R. P. Turco, O. B. Toon, T. P. Ackerman, J. B. Pollack and Carl Sagan. From the last names of the authors, this work is generally referred to as "TTAPS."]

We knew that nuclear explosions, particularly groundbursts, would lift an enormous quantity of fine soil particles into the atmosphere (more than 100,000 tons of fine dust for every megaton exploded in a surface burst). Our work was further spurred by Paul

Crutzen of the Max Planck Institute for Chemistry in Mainz, West Germany, and by John Birks of the University of Colorado, who pointed out that huge quantities of smoke would be generated in the burning of cities and forests following a nuclear war.

Groundbursts — at hardened missile silos, for example —generate fine dust. Airbursts — over cities and unhardened military installations — make fires and therefore smoke. The amount of dust and soot generated depends on the conduct of the war, the yields of the weapons employed and the ratio of groudbursts to airbursts. So we ran computer models for several dozen different nuclear war scenarios. Our baseline case, as in many other studies, was a 5000-megaton war with only a modest fraction of the yield (20 percent) expended on urban or industrial targets. Our job, for each case, was to follow the dust and smoke generated, see how much sunlight was absorbed and by how much the temperatures changed, figure out how the particles spread in longitude and latitude, and calculate how long before it all fell out of the air back onto the surface. Since the radioactivity would be attached to these same fine particles, our calculations also revealed the extent and timing of the subsequent radioactive fallout.

Some of what I am about to describe is horrifying. I know, because if horrifies me. There is a tendency — psychiatrists call it "denial" — to put it out of our minds, not to think about it. But if we are to deal intelligently, wisely, with the nuclear arms race, then we must steel ourselves to contemplate the horrors of nuclear war.

The results of our calculations astonished us. In the baseline case, the amount of sunlight at the ground was reduced to a few percent of normal — much darker, in daylight, than in a heavy overcast and too dark for plants to make a living from photosynthesis. At least in the Northern Hemisphere, where the great preponderance of strategic targets lies, an unbroken and deadly gloom would persist for weeks.

Even more unexpected were the temperatures calculated. In the baseline case, land temperatures, except for narrow strips of coastline, dropped to minus 25° Celsius (minus 13° Fahrenheit) and stayed below freezing for months — even for a summer war. (Because the atmospheric structure becomes much more stable as the upper atmosphere is heated and the lower air is cooled, we may have severely *underestimated* how long the cold and the dark would last.) The oceans, a significant heat reservoir, would not freeze, however, and a major ice age would probably not be triggered. But because the temperatures would drop so catastrophically, virtually all crops and farm animals, at least in the Northern Hemisphere, would be destroyed, as would most varieties of uncultivated or undomesticated food supplies. Most of the human survivors would starve.

In addition, the amount of radioactive fallout is much more than expected. Many previous calculations simply ignored the intermediate, time-scale fallout. That is, calculations were made for the prompt fallout — the plumes of radioactive debris blown downwind from each target — and for the long-term fallout the fine radioactive particles lofted into the stratosphere that would descend about a year later, after most of the radioactivity had decayed. However the radioactivity carried into the upper atmosphere (but not as high as the stratosphere) seems to have been largely forgotten. We found for the baseline case that roughly 30 percent of the land at northern midlatitudes could receive a radioactive dose greater than 250 rads, and that about 50 percent of northern mid latitudes could receive a dose greater than 100 rads. A 100-rad dose is the equivalent of about 1000 medical X-rays. A 400-rad dose will, more likely than not, kill you.

The cold, the dark and the intense radioactivity, together lasting for months, represent a severe assault on our civilization and our species. Civil and sanitary services would be wiped out. Medical facilities, drugs, the most rudimentary means for relieving the vast human suffering, would be unavailable. Any but the most elaborate shelters would be useless, quite apart from the question of what good it might be to emerge a few months later. Synthetics burned in the destruction of the cities would produce a wide variety of toxic gases, including carbon monoxide, cyanides, dioxins and furans. After the dust and soot settled out, the solar ultraviolet flux would be much larger than its present value. Immunity to disease would decline. Epidemics and pandemics would be rampant, especially after the billion or so unburied bodies began to thaw. Moreover, the combined influence of these severe and simultaneous stresses on life are likely to produce even more adverse consequences — biologists call them synergisms — that we are not yet wise enough to foresee.

So far, we have talked only of the Northern Hemisphere. But it now seems — unlike the case of a single nuclear weapons test — that in a real nuclear war, the heating of the vast quantities of atmospheric dust and soot in northern midlatitudes will transport these fine particles toward and across the Equator. We see just this happening in Martian dust storms. The Southern Hemisphere would experience effects that, while less severe than in the Northern Hemisphere, are nevertheless extremely ominous. The illusion with which some people in the Hemisphere reassure themselves — catching an Air New Zealand flight in a time of serious international crisis, or the like — is now much less tenable, even on the narrow issue of personal survival for those with the price of a ticket.

But what if nuclear wars can be contained, and much less than 5000 megatons is detonated? Perhaps the greatest surprise in our work was that even small nuclear wars can have devastating climatic effects. We considered a war in which a mere 100 megatons were exploded, less than one percent of the world arsenals, and only in low-yield airbursts over cities. This scenario, we found, would ignite thousands of fires, and the smoke from these fires alone would be enough to generate an epoch of cold and dark almost as severe as in the 5000 megaton case. The threshold for what Richard Turco has called the Nuclear Winter is very low.

Could we have overlooked some important effect? The carrying of dust and soot from the Northern to the Southern Hemisphere (as well as more local atmospheric circulation) will certainly thin the clouds out over the Northern Hemisphere. But, in many cases, this thinning would be insufficient to render the climatic consequences tolerable — and every time it got better in the Northern Hemisphere, it would get worse in the Southern.

Our results have been carefully scrutinized by more than 100 scientists in the United States, Europe and the Soviet Union. There are still arguments on points of detail. But the overall conclusion seems to be agreed upon: There are severe and previously unanticipated global consequences of nuclear war — subfreezing temperatures in a twilit radioactive gloom lasting for months or longer.

Scientists initially underestimated the effects of fallout, were amazed that nuclear explosions in space disabled distant satellites, had no idea that the fireballs from high-yield thermonuclear explosions could deplete the ozone layer and missed altogether the possible climatic effects of nuclear dust and smoke. What else have we overlooked?

Nuclear war is a problem that can be treated only theoretically. It is not amenable to experimentation. Conceivably, we have left something important out of our analysis, and the effects are more modest than we calculate. On the other hand, it is also possible — and, from previous experience, even likely — that there are further adverse effects that no one has yet been wise enough to recognize: With billions of lives at stake, where does conservatism lie — in assuming that the results will be better than we calculate, or worse?

Many biologists, considering the nuclear winter that these calculations describe, believe they carry somber implications for life on Earth. Many species of plants and animals would become extinct. Vast numbers of surviving humans would starve to death. The delicate ecological relations that bind together organisms on Earth in a fabric of mutual dependency would be torn, perhaps irreparably. There is little question that our global civilization would be destroyed. The human population would be reduced to prehistoric levels, or less. Life for any survivors would be extremely hard. And there seems to be a real possibility of the extinction of the human species.

It is now almost 40 years since the invention of nuclear weapons. We have not yet experienced a global thermonuclear war— although on more than one occasion we have come tremulously close. I do not think our luck can hold forever. Men and machines are fallible, as recent events remind us. Fools and madmen do exist, and sometimes rise to power. Concentrating always on the near future, we have ignored the long-term consequences of our actions. We have placed our civilization and our species in jeopardy.

Fortunately, it is not yet too late. We can safeguard the planetary civilization and the human family if we so choose. There is no more important or more urgent issue.

THE ART OF POLITICAL LYING

Jonathan Swift (1667-1745)

Born in Dublin, Ireland. Famous for his *Gulliver's Travels* (1726), which shows Jonathan's desire to encourage people to read deeper and not take things for granted; and *A Modest Proposal* (1729), which calmly suggests one solution for both the problem of overpopulation and the growing numbers of undernourished people.

We are told the devil is the father of lies, and was a liar from the beginning; so that, beyond contradiction, the invention is old: and, which is more, his first Essay of it was purely political, employed in undermining the authority of his prince, and seducing a third part of the subjects from their obedience: for which he was driven down from heaven, where (as Milton expresses it) he had been viceroy of a great western province; and forced to exercise his talent in inferior regions among other fallen spirits, poor or deluded men, whom he still daily tempts to his own sin, and will ever do so, till he be chained in the bottomless pit.

But although the devil be the father of lies, he seems, like other great inventors, to have lost much of his reputation by the continual improvements that have been made upon him.

Who first reduced lying into an art, and adapted it to politics, is not so clear from history, although I have made some diligent inquiries. I shall therefore consider it only according to the modern system, as it has been cultivated these twenty years past in the southern part of our own island.

The poets tell us that, after the giants were overthrown by the gods, the earth in revenge produced her last offspring, which was Fame. And the fable is thus interpreted: that when tumults and seditions are quieted, rumours and false reports are plentifully spread through a nation. So that, by this account, lying is the last relief of a routed, earth-born, rebellious party in a state. But here the moderns have made great additions, applying this art to the gaining of power and preserving it, as well as revenging themselves after they have lost it; as the same instruments are made use of by animals to feed themselves when they are hungry, and to bite those that tread upon them.

But the same genealogy cannot always be admitted for political lying; I shall therefore desire to refine upon it, by adding some circumstances of its birth and parents. A political lie is sometimes born out of a discarded statesman's head, and thence delivered to be nursed slid dandled by the rabble. Sometimes it is produced a monster, and licked into shape: at other times it comes into the world completely formed, and is spoiled in the licking. It is often born an infant in the regular way, and requires time to mature it; and often it sees the light in its full growth, but dwindles away by degrees. Sometimes it is of noble birth, and sometimes the spawn of a stock jobber. Here it screams aloud at the opening of the womb, and there it is delivered with a whisper. I know a lie that now disturbs half the kingdom with its noise, [of] which, although too proud and great at present to own its parents, I can remember its whisperhood. To conclude the nativity of this monster; when it comes into the world without a sting it is still-born; and whenever it loses its sting it dies.

No wonder if an infant so miraculous in its birth should be destined for great adventures; and accordingly we see it has been the guardian spirit of a prevailing party for almost twenty years. It can conquer kingdoms without fighting, and sometimes with the loss of a battle. It gives and resumes employments; can sink a mountain to a mole-hill, and raise a mole-hill to a mountain; has presided for many years at committees of elections; can wash a blackmoor white; make a saint of an atheist, and a patriot of a profligate; can furnish foreign ministers with intelligence, and raise or let fall the credit of the nation. This goddess flies with a huge looking-glass in her hands, to dazzle the crowd, and make them see, according as she turns it, their ruin in their interest, and their interest in their ruin. In this glass you will behold your best friends, clad in coats powdered with *fleurs de lis* and triple crowns; their girdles hung round with chains, and beads, and wooden shoes; and your worst enemies adorned with the ensigns of liberty, property, indulgence, moderation, and a cornucopia in their hands. Her large wings, like those of a flying-fish, are of no use but while they are moist; she therefore dips them in mud, and, soaring aloft, scatters it in the eyes of the multitude, flying with great swiftness; but at every turn is forced to stoop in dirty ways for new supplies.

I have been sometimes thinking, if a man had the art of the second sight for seeing lies, as they have in Scotland for seeing spirits, how admirably he might entertain himself in this town, by observing the different shapes, sizes, and colours of those swarms of lies which buzz about the heads of some people, like flies about a horse's ears in summer; or those legions hovering every afternoon in Exchange-alley, enough to darken the air; or over a club of discontented grandees, and thence sent down in cargoes to be scattered at elections.

There is one essential point wherein a political liar differs from others of the faculty, that he ought to have but a short memory, which is necessary according to the various occasions he meets with every hour of differing from himself and swearing to both sides of a contradiction, as he finds the persons disposed with whom he has to deal. In describing the virtues and vices of mankind, it is convenient upon every article, to have some eminent person in our eye, from whom we copy our description. I have strictly observed this rule, and my imagination this minute represents before me a certain great man famous for this talent, to the constant practice of which he owes his twenty years' reputation of the most skilful head in England for the management of nice affairs. The superiority of his genius consists in nothing else but an inexhaustible fund of political lies, which he plentifully distributes every minute he speaks, and by an unparalleled generosity forgets, and consequently contradicts, the next half-hour. He never yet considered whether any proposition were true or false, but whether it were convenient for the present minute or company to affirm or deny it; so that, if you think fit to refine upon him by interpreting everything he says, as we do dreams, by the contrary, you are still to seek, and will find yourself equally deceived whether you believe or not: the only remedy is to suppose that you have heard some inarticulate sounds, without any meaning at all; and beside, that will take off the horror you might be apt to conceive at the oaths wherewith he perpetually tags both ends of every proposition; although, at the same time, I think he cannot with any justice be taxed with perjury when he invokes God and Christ, because he has often fairly given public notice to the world that he believes in neither.

Some people may think that such an accomplishment as this can be of no great use to the owner, or his party, after it has been often practised and is become notorious; but they are widely mistaken. Few lies carry the inventor's mark, and the most prostitute enemy to truth may spread a thousand without being known for the author: besides, as the vilest writer has his readers, so the greatest liar has his believers; and it often happens that, if a lie be believed only for an hour, it has done its work, and there is no farther occasion for it. Falsehood flies, and truth comes limping after it, so that when men come to be undeceived it is too late; the jest is over, and the tale has had its effect: like a man who has thought of a good repartee when the discourse is changed or the company parted; or like a physician who has found out an infallible medicine after the patient is dead.

Considering that natural disposition in many men to lie, and in multitudes to believe, I have been perplexed what to do with that maxim so frequent in everybody's mouth, that truth will at last prevail. Here has this island of ours, for the greatest part of twenty years, lain under the influence of such counsels and persons, whose principle and interest it was to corrupt our manners, blind our understanding, drain our wealth, and in time destroy our constitution both in church and state, and we at last were brought to the very brink of ruin; yet, by the means of perpetual misrepresentations, have never been able to distinguish between our enemies and friends. We have seen a great part of the nation's money got into the hands of those who, by their birth, education, and merit, could pretend no higher than to wear our liveries; while others, who, by their credit, quality, and fortune, were only able to give reputation and success to the Revolution, were not only laid aside as dangerous and useless, but loaded with the scandal of Jacobites, men of arbitrary principles, and pensioners to France; while truth, who is said to lie in a well, seemed now to be buried there under a heap of stones. But I remember it was a usual complaint among the Whigs, that the bulk of the landed men was not in their interests, which some of the wisest looked on as an ill omen; and we saw it was with the utmost difficulty that they could reserve a majority, while the court and ministry were on their side, till they had learned those admirable expedients for deciding elections and influencing distant boroughs by powerful motives from the city. But all this was mere force and constraint, however upheld by most dexterous artifice and management, until the people began to apprehend their properties, their religion, and the monarchy itself in danger; when we saw them greedily laying hold on the first occasion to interpose. But of this mighty change in the dispositions of the people I shall discourse more at large in some following paper: wherein I shall endeavour to undeceive, or discover those deluded or deluding persons who hope or pretend it is only a short madness in the vulgar, from which they may soon recover; whereas, I believe it will appear to be very different in its causes, its symptoms, and its consequences; and prove a great example to illustrate the maxim I lately mentioned, that truth (however sometimes late) will at last prevail.

Fifth Avenue, Uptown: A Letter from Harlem

James Baldwin (1924-1987)

One of the great African American writers; his essays and fiction reveal his intense interest in social concerns. Long an expatriate, Baldwin's early experiences, both as a preacher's son and as a preacher himself, contribute to the powerful rhythm of his prose. In this writing, Baldwin describes the dehumanizing effects of ghetto life in Harlem.

There is a housing project standing now where the house in which we grew up once stood, and one of those stunted city trees is snarling where our doorway used to be. This is on the rehabilitated side of the avenue. The other side of the avenue — for progress takes time — has not been rehabilitated yet and it looks exactly as it looked in the days when we sat with our noses pressed against the windowpane, longing to be allowed to go "across the street." The grocery store which gave us credit is still there, and there can be no doubt that it is still giving credit. The people in the project certainly need it — far more, indeed, than they ever needed the project. The last time I passed by, the Jewish proprietor was still standing among his shelves, looking sadder and heavier but scarcely any older. Farther down the block stands the shoe-repair store in which our shoes were repaired until reparation became impossible and in which, then, we bought all our "new" ones. The Negro proprietor is still in the window, head down, working at the leather.

These two, I imagine, could tell a long tale if they would (perhaps they would be glad to if they could), having watched so many, for so long, struggling in the fishhooks, the barbed wire, of this avenue.

The avenue is elsewhere the renowned and elegant Fifth. The area I am describing, which, in today's gang parlance, would be called "the turf," is bounded by Lenox Avenue on the west, the Harlem River on the east, 135th Street on the north, and 130th Street on the south. We never lived beyond these boundaries; this is where we grew up. Walking along 145th Street — for example — familiar as it is, and similar, does not have the same impact because I did not know any of the people on the block. But when I turn east on 131st Street and Lenox Avenue, there is first a soda-pop joint, then a shoeshine "parlor," then a grocery store, then a dry cleaners', then the houses. All along the street there are people who watched me grow up, people who grew up with me, people I watched grow up along with my brothers and sisters: and, sometimes in my arms, sometimes underfoot, sometimes at my shoulder — or on it — their children, a riot, a forest of children, who include my nieces and nephews.

When we reach the end of this long block, we find ourselves on wide, filthy, hostile Fifth Avenue, facing that project which hangs over the avenue like a monument to the folly, and the cowardice, of good intentions. All along the block, for anyone who knows it, are immense human gaps, like craters. These gaps are not created merely by those who have moved away, inevitably into some other ghetto; or by those who have risen, almost always into a greater capacity for self-loathing and self-delusion; or yet by those who, by whatever means — War II, the Korean war, a policeman's gun or billy, a gang war, a brawl, madness, an overdose of heroin, or, simply, unnatural exhaustion — are dead. I am talking about those who are left, and I am talking principally about the young. What are they doing? Well, some, a minority, are fanatical churchgoers, members of the more extreme of the Holy Roller sects. Many, many more are "moslems," by affiliation or sympathy, that is to say that they are united by nothing more — and nothing less — than a hatred of the white world and all its works. They are present, for example, at every Buy Black street-corner meeting — meetings in which the speaker urges his hearers to cease trading with white men and establish a separate economy. Neither the speaker nor his hearers can possibly do this, of course, since Negroes do not own General Motors or RCA or the A&P, nor, indeed, do they own more than a wholly insufficient fraction of anything else in Harlem (those who *do* own anything are more interested in their profits than in their fellows). But these meetings nevertheless keep alive in the participators a certain pride of bitterness without which, however futile this bitterness may be, they could scarcely remain alive at all. Many have given up. They stay home and watch the

TV screen, living on the earnings of their parents, cousins, brothers, or uncles, and only leave the house to go to the movies or to the nearest bar. "How're you making it?" one may ask, running into them along the block, or in the bar. "Oh, I'm TVing it"; with the saddest, sweetest, most (shame-faced of smiles, and from a great distance. This distance one is compelled to respect; anyone who has traveled so far will not easily be dragged again into the world. There are further retreats, of course, than the TV screen or the bar. There are those who are simply sitting on their stoops, "stoned," animated for a moment only, and hideously, by the approach of someone who may lend them the money for a "fix." Or by the approach of someone from whom they can purchase it, one of the shrewd ones, on the way to prison or just coming out.

And the others, who have avoided all of these deaths, get up in the morning and go downtown to meet "the man." The work in the white man's world all day and come home in the evening to this fetid block. They struggle to instill in their children some private sense of honor or dignity which will help the child survive. This means, of course, that they must struggle, stolidly, incessantly, to keep this sense alive in themselves, in spite of the insults, the indifference, and the cruelty they are certain to encounter in their working day. They patiently browbeat the landlord into fixing the heat, the plaster, the plumbing; this demands prodigious patience; nor is patience usually enough. In trying to make their hovels habitable, they are perpetually throwing good money after bad. Such frustration, so long endured, is driving many strong, admirable men and women whose only crime is color to the very gates of paranoia.

One remembers them from another time — playing handball in the playground, going to church, wondering if they were going to be promoted at school. One remembers them going off to war — gladly, to escape this block. One remembers their return. Perhaps one remembers their wedding day. And one sees where the girl is now — vainly looking for salvation from some other embittered, trussed, and struggling boy — and sees the all-but-abandoned children in the streets.

Now I am perfectly aware that there are other slums in which white men are fighting for their lives, and mainly losing. I know that blood is also flowing through those streets and that the human damage there is incalculable. People are continually pointing out to me the wretchedness of white people in order to console me for the wretchedness of blacks. But an itemized account of the American failure does not console me and it should not console anyone else. That hundreds of thousands of white people are living, in effect, no better than the "niggers" is not a fact to be regarded with complacency. The social and moral bankruptcy suggested by this fact is of the bitterest, most terrifying kind.

The people, however, who believe that this democratic anguish has some consoling value are always pointing out that So-and-So, white, and So-and-So, black, rose from the slums into the big time. The existence — the public existence — of, say, Frank Sinatra and Sammy Davis, Jr. proves to them that America is still the land of opportunity and that inequalities vanish before the determined will.

It proves nothing of the sort. The determined will is rare — at the moment, in this country, it is unspeakably rare — and the inequalities suffered by the many are in no way justified by the rise of a few. A few have always risen — in every country, every era, and in the teeth of regimes which can by no stretch of the imagination be thought of as free. Not all of these people, it is worth remembering, left the world better than they found it. The determined will is rare, but it is not invariably benevolent. Furthermore, the American equation of success with the big times reveals an awful disrespect for human life and human achievement. This equation has placed our cities among the most dangerous in the world and has placed our youth among the most empty and most bewildered. The situation of our youth is not mysterious. Children have never been very good at listening to their elders, but they have never failed to imitate them. They must, they have no other models. That is exactly what our children are doing. They are imitating our immortality, our disrespect for the pain of others.

All other slum dwellers, when the bank account permits it, can move out of the slum and vanish altogether from the eye of persecution. No Negro in this country has ever made that much money and it will be a long time before any Negro does. The Negroes in Harlem, who have no money, spend what they have on such gimcracks as they are sold. These include "wider" TV screens, more "faithful" hi-fi sets, more "powerful" cars, all of which, of course, are obsolete long before they are paid for. Anyone who has ever struggled with poverty knows how extremely expensive it is to be poor; and if one is a member of a captive population, economically speaking, one's feet have placed on the treadmill forever. One is victimized, economically, in a thousand ways — rent, for example, or car insurance. Go shopping one day in Harlem — for anything — and compare Harlem prices and quality with those downtown.

The people who have managed to get off this block have only got as far as a more respectable ghetto. This respectable getto does not even have the advantages of the disreputable one — friends, neighbors, a familiar church, and friendly tradesmen; and it is not, moreover, in the nature of any ghetto to remain respectable long. Every Sunday, people who have left the block take the lonely ride back, draging their increasingly discontented children with them. They spend the day talking, not always with words, about the trouble they've seen and the trouble — one must watch their eyes as they watch their children — they are only too likely to see. For children do not like ghettos. It takes them nearly no time to discover exactly why they are there.

The projects in Harlem are hated. They are hated almost as much as policemen, and this is saying a great deal. And they are hated for the same reason: both reveal, unbearably, the real attitude of the white world, no matter how many liberal speeches are made, no matter how many lofty editorials are written, no matter how many civil-rights commissions are set up.

The projects are hideous, of course, there being a law, apparently respected throughout the world, that popular housing shall be as cheerless as a prison. They are jumped all over Harlem, colorless, bleak, high, and revolting. The wide windows look out on Harlem's invincible and indescribable squalor: the Park Avenue railroad tracks, around which, about forty years ago, the present dark community began: the unrehabilitated houses, bowed down, it would seem, under the great weight of the frustration and bitterness they contain; the dark, the ominous schoolhouses from which the child may emerge maimed, blinded, hooked, or engaged for life: and the churches, churches, block upon block of churches, niched in the walls like cannon in the walls of a fortress. Even if the administration of the projects were not so insanely humiliating (for example: one must report raises in salary to the management, which will then eat up the profit by raising one's rent: the management has the right to know who is staying in your apartment: the management can ask you to leave, at their discretion), the projects would still be hated because they are an insult to the meanest intelligence.

Harlem got its first private project, Riverton — which is now, naturally, a slum — about twelve years ago because at that time Negroes were not allowed to live in Stuyvesant Town. Harlem watched Riverton go up, therefore in the most violent bitterness of spirit, and hated it long before the builders arrived. They began hating it at about the time people began moving out of their condemned houses to make room for this additional proof of how thoroughly the white world despised them. And they had scarcely moved in, naturally, before they began smashing windows, defacing walls, urinating in the elevators, and fornicating in the playgrounds.

Liberals, both white and black, were appalled at the spectacle. I was appalled by the liberal innocence — or cynicism, which comes out in practice as much the same thing. Other people were delighted to be able to point to proof positive that nothing could be done to better the lot of the colored people. They were, and are, right in one respect: that nothing can be done as long as they are treated like colored people. The people in Harlem know they are living there because white people do not think they are good enough to live anywhere else. No amount of "improvement" can sweeten this fact. Whatever money is now being earmarked to improve this, or any other ghetto, might as well be burnt. A ghetto can be improved in one way only: out of existence.

Similarly, the only way to police a ghetto is to be oppressive. None of the Police Commissioner's men, even with the best will in the world, have any way of understanding the lives led by the people they swagger about in twos and threes controlling. Their very presence is an insult, and it would be, even if they spent their entire day feeding gumdrops to children. They represent the force of the white world, and the world's real intentions are, simply for the world's criminal profit and ease, to keep the black man corraled up here, in his place. The badge, the gun in the holster, and the swinging club make vivid what will happen should his rebellion become overt. Rare, indeed, is the Harlem citizen, from the most circumspect church member to the most shiftless adolescent, who does not have a long tale to tell of police incompetence, injustice, or brutality. I myself have witnessed and endured it more than once. The businessmen and racketeers also have a story. And so do the prostitutes. (And this is not, perhaps, the place to discuss Harlem's very complex attitude toward black policemen, nor the reasons, according to Harlem, that they are nearly all downtown.)

It is hard, on the other hand, to blame the policeman, blank, good-natured, thoughtless, and insuperably innocent, for being such a perfect representative of the people he serves. He, too, believes in good intentions and is astounded and offended when they are not taken for the deed. He has never, himself, done anything for which to be hated — which of us has? — and yet he is facing, daily and nightly, people who would gladly see him dead, and he knows it. There is no way for him not to know it: there are few things under heaven more unnerving than the silent, accumulating contempt and hatred of a people. He moves through Harlem, therefore, like an occupying soldier in a bitterly hostile country; which is precisely what, and where, he is, and is the reason he walks in twos and threes. And he is not the only one who knows why he is always in company: the people who are watching him know why, too. Any street meeting, sacred or secular, which he and his colleagues uneasily cover has as its explicit or implicit burden the cruelty and injustice of the white domination. And these days, of course, in terms increasingly vivid and jubilant, it speaks of the end of that domination. The white policeman standing on a Harlem street corner finds himself at the very center of the revolution now occurring in the world. He is not prepared for it — naturally, nobody is — and, what is possibly much more to the point, he is exposed, as few white people are, to the anguish of the black people around him. Even if he is gifted with the merest mustard grain of imagination, something must seep in. He cannot avoid observing that some of the children, in spite of their color, remind him of children he has known and loved, perhaps even of his own children. He knows that he certainly does not want *his* children living this way. He can retreat from his uneasiness in only one direction: into a callousness which very shortly becomes second nature. He becomes more callous, the population becomes more hostile, the situation grows more tense, and the police force is increased. One day, to everyone's astonishment, someone drops a match in the powder keg and everything blows up. Before the dust has settled or the blood congealed, editorials, speeches, and civil-rights commissions are loud in the land, demanding to know what happened. What happened is that Negroes want to be treated like men.

Negroes want to be treated like men: a perfectly straightforward statement, containing only seven words. People who have mastered Kant, Hegel, Shakespeare, Marx, Freud, and the Bible find this statement utterly impenetrable. The idea seems to threaten profound, barely conscious assumptions. A kind of panic paralyzes their features, as though they found themselves trapped on the edge of a steep place. I once tried to describe to a very well-known American intellectual the conditions among Negroes in the South. My recital disturbed him and made him indignant; and he asked me in perfect innocence, "Why don't all the Negroes in the South move North?"

I tried to explain what *has* happened, unfailingly, whenever a significant body of Negroes move North. They do not escape Jim Crow: they merely encounter another, not-less-deadly variety. They do not move to Chicago, they move to the South Side; they do not move to New York, they move to Harlem. The pressure within the ghetto causes the ghetto walls to expand, and this expansion is always violent. White people hold the line as long as they can, and in as many ways as they can, from verbal intimidation to physical violence. But inevitably the border which has divided the ghetto from the rest of the world falls into the hands of the ghetto. The white people fall back bitterly before the black horde; the landlords make a tidy profit by raising the rent, chopping up the rooms, and all but dispensing with the upkeep; and what has once been a neighborhood turns into a "turf." This is precisely what happened when the Puerto Ricans arrived in their thousands — and the bitterness thus caused is, as I write, being fought out all up and down those streets.

Northerners indulge in an extremely dangerous luxury. They seem to feel that because they fought on the right side during the Civil War, and won, they have earned the right merely to deplore what is going on in the South, without taking any responsibility for it; and that they can ignore what is happening in Northern cities because what is happening in Little Rock or Birmingham is worse. Well, in the first place, it is not possible for anyone who has not endured both to know which is "worse." I know Negroes who prefer the South and white Southerners, because "At least there, you haven't got to play any guessing games!" The guessing games referred to have driven more than one Negro into the narcotics ward, the madhouse, or the river. I know another Negro, a man very dear to me, who says with conviction and with truth, "The spirit of the South is the spirit of America." He was born in the North and did his military training in the South. He did not, as far as I can gather, find the South "worse"; he found it, if anything, all too familiar. In the second place, though, even if Birmingham *is* worse, no doubt Johannesburg, South Africa, beats it by several miles, and Buchenwald was one of the worst things that ever happened in the entire history of the world. The world has never lacked for horrifying examples; but I do not believe that these examples are meant to be used as justification for our own crimes. This perpetual justification empties the heart of all human feeling. The emptier our hearts become, the greater will be our crimes. Thirdly, the South is not merely an embarrassingly backward region, but a part of this country, and what happens there concerns every one of us.

As far as the color problem is concerned, there is but one difference between the Southern white and the Northerner: the Southerner remembers, historically and in his own psyche, a kind of Eden in which he loved black people and they loved him. Historically, the flaming sword laid across this Eden is the Civil War. Personally, it is the Southerner's sexual coming of age, when, without any warning, unbreakable taboos are set up between himself and his past. Everything, thereafter, is permitted him except the love he remembers and has never ceased to need. The resulting, indescribable torment affects every Southern mind and is the basis of the Southern hysteria.

None of this is true for the Northerner. Negroes represent nothing to him personally, except, perhaps, the dangers of carnality. He never sees Negroes. Southerners see them all the time. Northerners never think about them whereas Southerners are never really thinking of anything else. Negroes are, therefore, ignored in the North and are under surveillance in the South, and suffer hideously in both places. Neither the Southerner nor the Northerner is able to look on the Negro simply as a man. It seems to be indispensable to the national self-esteem that the Negro be considered either as a kind of ward (in which case we are told how many Negroes, comparatively, bought Cadillac last year and how few, comparatively, were lynched), or as a victim (in which case we are promised that he will never vote in our assemblies or go to school with our kids). They are two sides of the same coin and the South will not change — *cannot* change — until the North changes. The country will not change until it re-examines itself and discovers what it really means by freedom. In the meantime, generations keep being born, bitterness is increased by incompetence, pride, and folly, and the world shrinks around us.

It is a terrible, an inexorable, law that one cannot deny the humanity of another without diminishing one's own: in the face of one's victim, one sees oneself. Walk through the streets of Harlem and see what we, this nation, have become.

TEENAGE WASTELAND

Anne Tyler (**1941-**)

Born in Minneapolis, Minnesota, grew up in Raleigh, North Carolina, and thinks of herself a Southerner. A graduate of Duke University, she has done graduate work in Russian studies at Columbia University. Many of Tyler's short stories have appeared in magazines and she has written a number of novels, one of which, *The Accidental Tourist* (1985) was made into a film. This story was originally published in Seventeen (1984), tells of the troubled Coble family.

He used to have very blond hair — almost white — cut shorter than other children's so that on his crown a little cowlick always stood up to catch the light. But this was when he was small. As he grew older, his hair grew darker, and he wore it longer — past his collar even. It hung in lank, taffy-colored ropes around his face, which was still an endearing face, fine-featured, the eyes an unusual aqua blue. But his cheeks, of course, were no longer round, and a sharp new Adam's apple jogged in his throat when he talked.

In October, they called from the private school he attended to request a conference with his parents. Daisy went alone; her husband was at work. Clutching her purse, she sat on the principal's couch and learned that Donny was noisy, lazy, and disruptive: always fooling around with his friends, and he wouldn't respond in class.

In the past, before her children were born, Daisy had been a fourth-grade teacher. It shamed her now to sit before this principal as a parent, a delinquent parent, a parent who struck Mr. Lanham, no doubt, as unseeing or uncaring. "It isn't that we're not concerned," she said. "Both of us are. And we've done what we could, whatever we could think of. We don't let him watch TV on school nights. We don't let him talk on the phone till he's finished his homework. But he tells us he doesn't *have* any homework or he did it all in study hall. How are we to know what to believe?"

From early October through November, at Mr. Lanham's suggestion, Daisy checked Donny's assignments every day. She sat next to him as he worked, trying to be encouraging, sagging inwardly as she saw the poor quality of everything he did — the sloppy mistakes in math, the illogical leaps in his English themes, the history questions left blank if they required any research.

Daisy was often late starting supper, and she couldn't give as much attention to Donny's younger sister. "You'll never guess what happened at..." Amanda would begin, and Daisy would have to tell her, "Not now, honey."

By the time her husband, Matt, came home, she'd be snappish. She would recite the day's hardships — the fuzzy instructions in English, the botched history map, the morass of unsolvable algebra equations. Matt would look surprised and confused, and Daisy would gradually wind down. There was no way, really, to convey how exhausting all this was.

In December, the school called again. This time, they wanted Matt to come as well. She and Matt had to sit on Mr. Lanham's couch like two bad children and listen to the news: Donny had improved only slightly, raising a D in history to a C, and a C in algebra to a B-minus. What was worse, he had developed new problems. He had cut classes on at least three occasions. Smoked in the furnace room. Helped Sonny Barnett break into a freshman's locker. And last week, during athletics, he and three friends had been seen off the school grounds; when they returned, the coach had smelled beer on their breath.

Daisy and Matt sat silent, shocked. Matt rubbed his forehead with his fingertips. Imagine, Daisy thought, how they must look to Mr. Lanham: an overweight housewife in a cotton dress and a too-tall, too-thin insurance agent in a baggy, frayed suit. Failures, both of them — the kind of people who are always hurrying to catch up, missing the point of things that everyone else grasps at once. She wished she'd worn nylons instead of knee socks.

It was arranged that Donny would visit a psychologist for testing. Mr. Lanham knew just the person. He would set this boy straight, he said.

When they stood to leave, Daisy held her stomach in and gave Mr. Lanham a firm, responsible handshake.

Donny said the Psychologist was a jackass and the tests were really dumb; but he kept all three of his appointments, and when it was time for the follow-up conference with the psychologist and both parents, Donny combed his hair and seemed unusually sober and subdued. The psychologist said Donny had no serious emotional problems. He was merely going through a difficult period in his life. He required some academic help and a better sense of self-worth. For this reason, he was suggesting a man named Calvin Beadle, a tutor with considerable psychological training.

In the car going home, Donny said he'd be damned if he'd let them drag him to some stupid fairy tutor. His father told him to watch his language in front of his mother.

That night, Daisy lay awake pondering the term "self-worth." She had always been free with her praise. She had always told Donny he had talent, was smart, was good with his hands. She had made a big to-do over every little gift he gave her. In fact, maybe she had gone too far, although, Lord knows, she had meant every word. Was that his trouble?

She remembered when Amanda was born. Donny had acted lost and bewildered. Daisy had been alert to that, of course, but still, a new baby keeps you so busy. Had she really done all she could have? She longed — she ached — for a time machine. Given one more chance, she'd do it perfectly — hug him more, praise him more, or perhaps praise him less. Oh, who can say . . .

The tutor told Donny to call him Cal. All his kids did, he said. Daisy thought for a second that he meant his own children, then realized her mistake. He seemed too young, anyhow, to be a family man. He wore a heavy brown handlebar mustache. His hair was as long and stringy, as Donny's, and his jeans as faded. Wire-rimmed spectacles slid down his nose. He lounged in a canvas director's chair with his fingers laced across his chest, and he casually, amiably questioned Donny, who sat upright and glaring in an armchair.

"So they're getting on your back at school," said Cal. "Making a big deal about anything you do wrong."

"Right," said Donny.

"Any idea why that would be?"

"Oh, well, you know, stuff like homework and all," Donny said.

"You don't do your homework?"

"Oh, well, I might do it sometimes but not just exactly like they want it." Donny sat forward and said, "It's like a prison there, you know? You've got to go to every class, you can never step off the school grounds."

"You cut classes sometimes?"

"Sometimes," Donny said, with a glance at his parents.

Cal didn't seem perturbed. "Well," he said, "I'll tell you what. Let's you and me try working together three nights a week. Think you can handle that? We'll see if we can show that school of yours a thing or two. Give it a month; then if you don't like it, we'll stop. If *I* don't like it, we'll stop. I mean. sometimes people just don't get along, right? What do you say to that?"

"Okay," Donny said. He seemed pleased.

"Make it seven o'clock till eight, Monday, Wednesday, and Friday," Cal told Matt and Daisy. They nodded. Cal shambled to his feet, gave them a little salute, and showed them to the door.

This was where he lived as well as worked, evidently. The

interview had taken place in the dinning room, which had been transformed into a kind of office. Passing the living room, Daisy winced at the rock music she had been hearing, without registering it, ever since she had entered the house. She looked in and saw a boy about Donny's age lying on a sofa with a book. Another boy and a girl were playing Ping-Pong in front of the fireplace. "You have several here together?" Daisy asked Cal.

"Oh, sometimes they stay on after their sessions, just to rap. They're a pretty sociable group, all in all Plenty of goof-offs like young Donny here."

He cuffed Donny's shoulder playfully. Donny flushed and grinned.

Climbing into the car, Daisy asked Donny, "Well? What do you think?"

But Donny had returned to his old evasive self. he jerked his chin toward the garage. "Look," he said. "He's got a basketball net."

Now on Mondays, Wednesdays, and Fridays, they had supper early — the instant Matt came home. Sometimes, they had to leave before they were really finished. Amanda would still be eating her dessert. "Bye, honey. Sorry," Daisy would tell her.

Cal's first bill sent a flutter of panic through Daisy's chest, but it was worth it, of course. Just look at Donny's face when they picked him up: alight and full of interest. The principal telephoned Daisy, to tell her how Donny had improved. "Of course, it hasn't shown up in his grades yet, but several of the teachers have noticed how his attitude's changed. Yes, sir, I think we're onto something here."

At home, Donny didn't act much different. He still seemed to have a low opinion of his parents. But Daisy supposed that was unavoidable — part of being fifteen. He said his parents were too "controlling" — a word that made Daisy give him a sudden look. He said they acted like wardens. On weekends, they enforced a curfew. And any time he went to a party, they always telephoned first to see if adults would be supervising. "For God's sake!" he said. "Don't you trust me?"

"It isn't a matter of trust, honey. . ." But there was no explaining to him.

His tutor called one afternoon. "I get the sense," he said, "that this kid's feeling . . . underestimated, you know? Like you folks expect the worst of him. I'm thinking we ought to give him more rope."

"But see, he's still so suggestible," Daisy said. "When his friends suggest some mischief — smoking or drinking or such — why, he just finds it hard not to go along with them."

"Mrs. Coble" the tutor said, "I think, this kid is hurting. You know? Here's serious, sensitive kid, telling you he'd like to take on some grown-up challenges, and you're giving him the message that he can't be trusted. Don't you understand how that hurts?"

"Oh," said Daisy.

"It undermines his self-esteem — don't you realize that?"

"Well, I guess you're right," said Daisy. She saw Donny

suddenly from a whole new angle: his pathetically poor posture, that slouch so forlorn that his shoulders seemed about to meet his chin. . . oh, wasn't it awful being young? She'd had a miserable adolescence herself and had always sworn no child of hers would ever be that unhappy.

They let Donny stay out later, they didn't call ahead to see if the parties were supervised, and they were careful not to grill him about his evening. The tutor had set down so many rules! They were not allowed any questions at all about any aspect of school, nor were they to speak with his teachers. If a teacher had some complaint, she should phone Cal. Only one teacher disobeyed — the history teacher, Miss Evans. She called one morning in February. "I'm a little concerned about Donny, Mrs. Coble."

"Oh, I'm sorry, Miss Evans, but Donny's tutor handles these things now. . ."

"I always deal directly with the parents. You are the parent," Miss Evans said, speaking very slowly and distinctly. "Now, here is the problem. Back when you were helping Donny with his homework, his grades rose from a D to a C, but now they've slipped back, and they're closer to an F."

"They are?"

"I think you should start overseeing his homework again."

"But Donny's tutor says . . ."

"It's nice that Donny has a tutor, but you should still be in charge of his homework. With you, he learned it. Then he passed his tests. With the tutor, well, it seems the tutor is more of a crutch. 'Donny,' I say, 'a quiz is coming up on Friday. Hadn't you better be listening instead of talking?' 'That's okay, Miss Evans,' he says. 'I have a tutor now.' Like a talisman! I really think you ought to take over, Mrs. Coble."

"I see," said Daisy. "Well, I'll think about that. Thank you for calling."

Hanging up, she felt a rush of anger at Donny. A talisman! For a talisman, she'd given up all luxuries, all that time with her daughter, her evenings at home!

She dialed Cal's number. He sounded muzzy. "I'm sorry if I woke you," she told him, "but Donny's history teacher just called. She says he isn't doing well."

"She should have dealt with me."

"She wants me to start supervising his homework again. His grades are slipping."

"Yes," said the tutor, "but you and I both know there's more to it than mere grades, don't we? I care about the *whole* child — his happiness, his self-esteem. The grades will come. Just give them time."

When she hung up, it was Miss Evans she was angry at. What a narrow woman!

It was Cal this, Cal that, Cal says this, Cal and I did that. Cal lent Donny an album by the Who. He took Donny and two other pupils to a rock concert. In March, when Donny began to talk endlessly on the phone with a girl named Miriam, Cal even let Miriam come to one of the tutoring sessions. Daisy was touched that Cal would grow so involved in Donny's life, but she was also a little hurt, because she had offered to have Miriam to dinner and Donny had refused. Now he asked them to drive her to Cal's house without a qualm.

This Miriam was an unappealing girl with blurry lipstick and masses of rough red hair. She wore a short, bulky jacket that would not have been out of place on a motorcycle. During the trip to Cal's she was silent, but coming back, she was more talkative. "What a neat guy and what a house! All those kids hanging out, like a club. And the stereo playing rock. . .gosh, he's not like a grown-up at all! Married and divorced and everything, but you'd think he was our own age."

"Mr. Beadle was married?" Daisy asked.

"Yeah, to this really controlling lady. She didn't understand him a bit."

"No, I guess not," Daisy said.

Spring came, and the students who hung around at Cal's drifted out to the basketball net above the garage. Sometimes, when Daisy and Matt arrived to pick up Donny, they'd find him there with the others — spiky and excited, jittering on his toes beneath the backboard. It was staying light much longer now, and the neighboring fence cast narrow bars across the bright grass. Loud music would be spilling from Cal's windows. Once it was the Who, which Daisy recognized from the time that Donny had borrowed the album. "*Teenage Wasteland*," she said aloud, identifying the song, and Matt gave a short, dry laugh. "It certainly is," he said. He'd misunderstood; he thought she was commenting on the scene spread before them. In fact, she might have been. The players looked like hoodlums, even her son. Why, one of Cal's students had recently been knifed in a tavern. One had been shipped off to boarding school in midterm; two had been withdrawn by their parents. On the other hand, Donny had mentioned someone who'd been studying with Cal for five years. "Five years!" said Daisy. Doesn't anyone ever stop needing him?"

Donny looked at her. Lately, whatever she said about Cal was read as criticism. "You're just feeling competitive," he said. "And controlling."

She bit her lip and said no more.

In April, the principal called to tell her that Donny had been expelled. There had been a locker check, and in Donny's locker they found five cans of beer and half a pack of cigarettes. With Donny's previous record, his offense meant expulsion.

Daisy gripped the receiver tightly and said, "Well, where is he now?"

"We've sent him home," said Mr. Lanham. "He's packed up all his belongings, and he's coming home on foot."

Daisy wondered what she would say to him. She felt him looming closer and closer, bringing this brand-new situation that no one had prepared her to handle. What other place would take him? Could they enter him in public school? What were the rules? She stood at the living room window, waiting for him to show up. Gradually, she realized that he was taking too long. She checked the clock. She stared up the street again.

When an hour had passed, she phoned the school. Mr. Lanham's secretary answered and told her in a grave, sympathetic voice that yes, Donny Coble had most definitely gone home. Daisy called her husband. He was out of the office. She went back to the window and thought awhile, and then she called Donny's tutor.

"Donny's been expelled from school," she said, "and now I don't know where he's gone. I wonder if you've heard from him?"

There was a long silence. "Donny's with me, Mrs. Coble," he finally said.

"With you? How'd he get there?

"He hailed a cab, and I paid the driver."

"Could I speak to him, please?"

There was another silence. "Maybe it'd be better if we had a conference," Cal said.

"I don't *want* a conference. I've been standing at the window picturing him dead or kidnapped or something, and now you tell me you want a — "

"Donny is very, very upset. Understandably so," said Cal. "Believe me, Mrs. Coble, this is not what it seems. Have you asked Donny's side of the story?"

"Well, of course not, how could I? He went running off to you instead."

"Because he didn't feel he'd be listened to."

"But I haven't even — "

"Why don't you come out and talk? The three of us," said Cal, "will try to get this thing in perspective."

"Well, all right," Daisy said. But she wasn't as reluctant as she sounded. Already, she felt soothed by the calm way Cal was taking this.

Cal answered the doorbell at once. He said, "Hi, there," and led her into the dining room. Donny sat slumped in a chair, chewing the knuckle of one thumb. "Hello, Donny," Daisy said. He flicked his eyes in her direction.

"Sit here, Mrs. Coble," said Cal, placing her opposite Donny. He himself remained standing, restlessly pacing. "So," he said.

Daisy stole a look at Donny. His lips were swollen, as if he'd been crying.

"You know," Cal told Daisy, "I kind of expected something like this. That's a very punitive school you've got him in — you realize that. And any half-decent lawyer will tell you they've violated his civil rights. Locker checks! Where's their search warrant?"

"But if the rule is — " Daisy said.

"Well, anyhow, let him tell you his side."

She looked at Donny. He said, "It wasn't my fault. I promise."

"They said your locker was full of beer."

"It was a put-up job! See, there's this guy that doesn't like me. He put all these beers in my locker and started a rumor going, so Mr. Lanham ordered a locker check."

"What was the boy's name?" Daisy asked.

"Huh?"

"Mrs. Coble, take my word, the situation is not so unusual," Cal said. "You can't imagine how vindictive kids can be sometimes."

"What was the boy's *name*," said Daisy, "so that I can ask Mr. Lanham if that's who suggested he run a locker check."

"You don't believe me," Donny said.

"And how'd this boy get your combination in the first place?"

"Frankly," said Cal, "I wouldn't be surprised to learn the school was in on it. Any kid that marches to a different drummer, why, they'd just love an excuse to get rid of him. The school is where I lay the blame."

"Doesn't *Donny* ever get blamed?"

"Now, Mrs. Coble, you heard what he — "

"Forget it," Donny told Cal. "You can see she doesn't trust me."

Daisy drew in a breath to say that of course she trusted him — a reflex. But she knew that bold-faced, wide-eyed look of Donny's. He had worn that look when he was small, denying some petty misdeed with the evidence plain as day all around him. Still, it was hard for her to accuse him outright. She temporized and said, "The only thing I'm sure of is that they've kicked you out of school, and now I don't know what we're going to do."

"We'll fight it," said Cal.

"We can't. Even you must see we can't."

"I could apply to Brantly," Donny said.

Cal stopped his pacing to beam down at him. "Brantly! Yes. They're really onto where a kid is coming from, at Brantly. Why, *I* could get into Brantly. I work with a lot of their students."

Daisy had never heard of Brantly, but already she didn't like it.

And she didn't like Cal's smile, which struck her now as feverish and avid — a smile of hunger.

On the fifteenth of April, they entered Donny in a public school, and they stopped his tutoring sessions. Donny fought both decisions bitterly. Cal, surprisingly enough, did not object. He admitted he'd made no headway with Donny and said it was because Donny was emotionally disturbed.

Donny went to his new school every morning, plodding off alone with his head down. He did his assignments, and he earned average grades, but he gathered no friends, joined no clubs. There was something exhausted and defeated about him.

The first week in June, during final exams, Donny vanished. He simply didn't come home one afternoon, and no one at school remembered seeing him. The police were reassuring, and for the first few days, they worked hard. They combed Donny's sad, messy room for clues; they visited Miriam and Cal. But then they started talking about the number of kids who ran away every year. Hundreds, just in this city. "He'll show up, if he wants to," they said. "If he doesn't, he won't."

Evidently, Donny didn't want to.

It's been three months now and still no word. Matt and Daisy still look for him in every crowd of awkward, heartbreaking teenage boys. Every time the phone rings, they imagine it might be Donny. Both parents have aged. Donny's sister seems to be staying away from home as much as possible.

At night, Daisy lies awake and goes over Donny's life. She is trying to figure out what went wrong, where they made their first mistake. Often, she finds herself blaming Cal, although she knows he didn't begin it. Then at other times she excuses him, for without him, Donny might have left earlier. Who really knows? In the end, she can only sigh and search for a cooler spot on the pillow. As she falls asleep, she occasionally glimpses something in the corner of her vision. It's something fleet and round, a ball — a basketball. It flies up, it sinks through the hoop, descends, lands in a yard littered with last year's leaves and striped with bars of sunlight as white as bones, bleached and parched and cleanly picked.

BEYOND THE MELTING POT

William A. Henry III

Someday soon, surely much sooner than most people . . . realize, white Americans will become a minority group. Long before that day arrives, the presumption that the "typical" U.S. citizen is someone who traces his or her descent in a direct line to Europe will be part of the past. By the time [today's] elementary [school] students . . . reach midlife, their diverse ethnic experience in the classroom will be echoed in neighborhoods and workplaces throughout the U.S.

Already 1 American in 4 defines himself or herself as Hispanic or nonwhite. If current trends in immigration and birth rates persist, the Hispanic population will have further increased an estimated 21%, the Asian presence about 22%, blacks almost 12%, and whites a little more than 2% when the 20th century ends. By 2020, a date no further into the future than John F. Kennedy's election is in the past, the number of U.S. residents who are Hispanic or nonwhite will have more than doubled, to nearly 115 million, while the white population will not be increasing at all. By 2056, when someone born today will be 66 years old, the "average" U.S. resident, as defined by Census statistics, will trace his or her decent to Africa, Asia, the Hispanic world, the Pacific Islands, Arabia — almost anywhere but white Europe.

While there may remain towns or outposts where even a black family will be something of an oddity, where English and Irish and German surnames will predominate, where a traditional (some will wistfully say "real") America will still be seen on almost every street corner, they will be only the vestiges of an earlier nation. The former majority will learn, as a normal part of everyday life, the meaning of the Latin slogan engraved on U.S. coins — E PLURIBUS UNUM, one formed from many.

Among the younger populations that go to school and provide new entrants to the work force, the change will happen sooner. In some places an America beyond the melting pot has already arrived. In New York State some 40% of elementary and secondary-school children belong to an ethnic minority. Within a decade, the proportion is expected to approach 50%. In California white pupils are already a minority. Hispanics (who, regardless of their complexion, generally distinguish themselves from both blacks and whites) account for 31.4% of public school enrollment, blacks add 8.9%, and Asians and others amount to 11% — for a nonwhite total of 51.3%. This finding is not only a reflection of white flight from desegregated public schools. Whites of all ages account for just 58% of California's population. In San Jose bearers of the Vietnamese surname Nguyen outnumber the Joneses in the telephone directory 14 columns to eight.

Nor is the change confined to the coasts. Some 12,000 Hmong refugees from Laos have settled in St. Paul. At some Atlanta low-rent apartment complexes that used to be virtually all black, social workers today need to speak Spanish. At the Sesame Hut restaurant in Houston, a Korean immigrant owner trains Hispanic immigrant workers to prepare Chinese-style food for a largely black clientele. The Detroit area has 200,000 people of Middle Eastern descent; some 1,500 small grocery and convenience stores in the vicinity are owned by a whole subculture of Chaldean Christians with roots in Iraq. "Once America was a microcosm of European nationalities," says Molefi Asante, chairman of the department of African-American studies at Temple University in Philadelphia. "Today America is a microcosm of the world."

History suggests that sustaining a truly multiracial society is difficult, or at least unusual. Only a handful of great powers of the distant past — Pharaonic Egypt and Imperial Rome, most notably — managed to maintain a distant national identity while embracing, and being ruled by, an ethnic mélange. The most ethnically diverse contemporary power, the Soviet Union, is beset with secessionist demands and near tribal conflicts. But such comparisons are flawed, because those empires were launched by conquest and maintained through an aggressive military presence. The U.S. was created, and continues to be redefined, primarily by voluntary immigration. This process has been one of the country's great strengths, infusing it with talent and energy. The "browsing of America" offers tremendous opportunity for capitalizing anew on the merits of many peoples from many lands. Yet this fundamental change in the ethnic makeup of the U.S. also poses risks. The American character is, resilient and thrives on change. But past periods of rapid evolution have also, alas, brought out deeper, more fearful aspects of national soul.

POLITICS: NEW AND SHIFTING ALLIANCES

A truly multiracial society will undoubtedly prove much harder to govern. Even seemingly race-free conflicts will be increasingly complicated by an overlay of ethnic tension. For example, the expected showdown in the early 21st century between the rising number of retirees and the dwindling number of workers who must be taxed to pay for the elders' Social Security benefits will probably be compounded by the fact that a large majority of recipients will be white, whereas a majority of workers paying for them will be nonwhite.

While prior generations of immigrants believed they had to learn English quickly to survive, many Hispanics now maintain that the Spanish language is inseparable from their ethnic and cultural identity, and seek to remain bilingual, if not primarily Spanish-speaking, for life. They see legislative drives to make English the sole official language, which have prevailed in some fashion in at least 16 states, as a political backlash. Says Arturo Vargas of the Mexican American Legal Defense and Educational Fund: "That's what English-only has been all about — a reaction to the growing population and influence of Hispanics. It's human nature to be uncomfortable with change. That's what the Census is all about, documenting changes and making sure the country keeps up."

Racial and ethnic conflict remains an ugly fact of American life everywhere, from working-class ghettos to college campuses, and those who do not raise their fists often raise their voices over affirmative action and other power sharing. When Florida Atlantic University, a state-funded institution under pressure to increase its low black enrollment, offered last month to give free tuition to every qualified black freshman who enrolled, the school was flooded with calls of complaint, some protesting that nothing was being done for "real" Americans. As the numbers of minorities increase, their demands for a share of the national bounty are bound to intensify, while whites are certain to feel ever more embattled. Businesses often feel whipsawed between immigration laws that punish them for hiring illegal aliens and anti-discrimination laws that penalize them for demanding excessive documentation from foreign-seeming job applicants. Even companies that consistently seek to do the right thing may be overwhelmed by the problems of diversifying a primarily white managerial corps fast enough to direct a work force that will be increasingly nonwhite and potentially, resentful.

Nor will tensions be limited to the polar simplicity of white vs. nonwhite. For all Jesse Jackson's rallying cries about shared goals, minority groups often feel keenly competitive. Chicago's Hispanic leaders have leapfrogged between white and black factions, offering support wherever there seemed to be the most to gain for their own community. Says Dan Solis of the Hispanic-oriented United Neighborhood Organization: "If you're thinking power, you don't put your eggs in one basket."

Blacks, who feel they waited longest and endured most in the fight for equal opportunity, are uneasy about being supplanted by Hispanics or, in some areas, by Asians as the numerically largest and most influential minority — and even more, about being outstripped in wealth and status by these newer groups. Because Hispanics are so numerous and Asians such a fast-growing group, they have become the "hot" minorities, and blacks feel their needs are getting lower priority. As affirmative action has broadened to include other groups — and to benefit white women perhaps most of all — blacks perceive it as having waned in value for them.

THE CLASSROOM: WHOSE HISTORY COUNTS?

Political pressure has already brought about sweeping change in public school textbooks over the past couple of decades and has begun to affect the core humanities curriculum at such élite universities as Standford. At stake at the college level is whether the traditional "canon" of Greek, Latin and West European humanities study should be expanded to reflect the cultures of Africa, Asia and other parts of the world. Many books treasured as classics by prior generations are now seen as tools of cultural imperialism. In the extreme form, this thinking rises to a value-deprived neutralism that views all cultures, regardless of the grandeur or paucity of their attainments, as essentially equal.

Even more troubling is a revisionist approach to history in which groups that have gained power in the present turn to remaking the past in the image of their desires. If 18th, 19th and earlier 20th century society should not have been so dominated by white Christian men of West European ancestry, they reason, then that past society should be reinvented as pluralist and democratic. Alternatively, the racism and sexism of the past are treated as inextricable from — and therefore irremediably tainting — traditional learning and values.

While debates over college curriculum get the most attention, professors generally can resist or subvert the most wrong-headed changes and students generally have mature enough judgment to sort out the arguments. Elementary- and secondary-school curriculums reach a far broader segment at a far more impressionable age, and political expediency more often wins over intellectual honesty. Exchanges have been vituperative in New York, where a state task force concluded that "African-Americans, Asian-Americans, Puerto Ricans and Native Americans have all been victims of an intellectual and educational oppression. . . . Negative characterizations, or the absence of positive references, have had a terribly damaging effect on the psyche of young people." In urging a revised syllabus, the task force argued, "Children from European culture will have a less arrogant perspective of being part of a group that has 'done it all.'" Many intellectuals are outraged. Political scientist Andrew

Hacker of Queens College lambastes a task-force suggestion that children be taught how "Native Americans were here to welcome new settlers from Holland, Senegal, England, Indonesia, France, the Congo, Italy, China, Iberia." Asks Hacker: "Did the Indians really welcome all those groups? Were they at Ellis Island when the Italians started to arrive? This is not history but a myth intended to bolster the self-esteem of certain children and, just possibly, a platform for advocates of various ethnic interests."

VALUES: SOMETHING IN COMMON

Economic and political issues, however much emotion they arouse, are fundamentally open to practical solution. The deeper significance of America's becoming a majority non-white society is what it means to the national psyche to individuals' sense of themselves and their nation — their idea of what it is to be American. People of color have often felt that whites treated equality as a benevolence granted to minorities rather than as an inherent natural right. Surely that condescension will wither.

Rather than accepting U.S. history and its meaning as settled, citizens will feel ever more free to debate where the nation's successes sprang from and what its unalterable beliefs are. They will clash over which myths and icons to invoke in education, in popular culture, in ceremonial speechmaking from political campaigns to the State of the Union address. Which is the more admirable heroism: the courageous holdout by a few conquest-minded whites over Hispanics at the Alamo, or the anonymous expression of hope by millions who filed through Ellis Island? Was the subduing of the West a daring feat of bravery and ingenuity, or a wretched example of white imperialism? Symbols deeply meaningful to one group can be a matter of indifference to another. Says University of Wisconsin chancellor Donna Shalala: "My grandparents came from Lebanon. I don't identify with the Pilgrims on a personal level." Christopher, Jencks, professor of sociology at Northwestern, asks, "Is anything more basic about turkeys and Pilgrims than about Martin Luther King and Selma? To me, it's six of one and half a dozen of the other, if children understand what it's like to be a dissident minority. Because the civil rights struggle is closer chronologically, it's likelier to be taught by someone who really cares."

Traditionalists increasingly distinguish between a "multi-racial" society, which they say would be fine, and a "multi-cultural" society, which they deplore. They argue that every society needs a universally accepted set of values and that new arrivals should therefore be pressured to conform to the mentality on which U.S. prosperity and freedom were built. Says Allan Bloom, author of the best-selling *The Closing of the American Mind*: "Obviously, the future of America can't be sustained if people keep only to their own ways and remain perpetual outsiders. The society has got to turn them into Americans. There are natural fears that today's immigrants may be too much of a cultural stretch for a nation based on Western values."

The counterargument, made by such scholars as historian Thomas Bender of New York University, is that if the center cannot hold, then one must redefine the center. It should be, he says, "the ever changing outcome of a continuing contest among social groups and ideas for the power to define public culture." Besides, he adds, many immigrants arrive committed to U.S. values; that is part of what attracted them. Says Julian Simon, professor of business administration at the University of Maryland: "The life and institutions here shape immigrants and not vice versa. This business about immigrants changing our institutions and our basic ways of life is hogwash. It's nativist scare talk."

CITIZENSHIP: FORGING A NEW IDENTITY

Historians note that Americans have felt before that their historical culture was being overwhelmed by immigrants, but conflicts between earlier-arriving English, Germans and Irish and later-arriving Italians and Jews did not have the obvious and enduring element of racial skin color. And there was never a time when the nonmainstream elements could claim, through sheer numbers, the potential to unite and exert political dominance. Says Bender: "The real question is whether or not our notion of diversity can successfully negotiate the color line."

For whites, especially those who trace their ancestry back to the early years of the Republic, the American heritage is a source of pride. For people of color, it is more likely to evoke anger and sometimes shame. The place where hope is shared is in the future. Demographer Ben Wattenberg, formerly perceived as a resister to social change, says "There's a nice chance that the American myth in the 1990s and beyond is going to ratchet another step toward this idea that we are the universal nation. That rings the bell of manifest destiny. We're a people with a mission and a sense of purpose, and we believe we have something to offer the world."

Not every erstwhile alarmist can bring himself to such optimism. Says Norman Podhoretz, editor of *Commentary*: "A lot of people are trying to undermine the foundations of the American experience and are pushing toward a more Balkanized society. I think that would be a disaster, not only because it would destroy a precious social inheritance but also because it would lead to enormous unrest, even violence."

While know-nothingism is generally confined to the more dismal corners of the .American psyche, it seems all too predictable that during the next decades many more mainstream white Americans will begin to speak openly about the nation they feel they are losing. There are not, after all, many nonwhite faces depicted in Norman Rockwell's paintings. White Americans are accustomed to thinking of themselves as the very picture of their nation. Inspiring as it may be to the rest of the world, significant as it may be to the U.S. role in global politics, world trade and the pursuit of peace, becoming a conspicuously multiracial society is bound to be a somewhat bumpy experience for many ordinary citizens. For older Americans, raised in a world where the numbers of whites were greater and the visibility of nonwhites was carefully restrained, the new world will seem ever stranger. But as children in . . . classrooms across the nation are coming to realize, the new world is here. It is now. And it is irreversibly the America to come.

Section IV: Women

Where the Boys Aren't

Brendan Koerner

Brendan Koerner was previously a Senior Editor at U.S. News & World Report, where he wrote more than 100 feature articles including six cover stories, since 1996 on subjects ranging from higher education to urban renewal to religion to business and technology. His stories have included *A Lust for Profits*, a cover-story, study of the Internet pornography industry, and *Can Hackers be Stopped*, a special report on information security.

Heels to Heaven, an a cappella group at the University of North Carolina-Chapel Hill, needed to add a few baritones and basses as the 1996-97 school year opened. But deep voices are in short supply on a campus that is over 60 percent female. In its quest for low-end sounds, the group conducted a public relations blitz, plastering every dorm with signs declaring "Real Men Sing Loud!"

The campaign worked, and it doubtless will be tried again in the future: With females accounting for 61 percent of the university's pool of applicants, the gender gap at Chapel Hill is unlikely to close soon. "There is an obvious lack of guys on campus," sighs Catherine Brandt, a junior and former member of Heels to Heaven. "I don't know what to say about it other than they're not there."

They're not there at Seattle Pacific University, either, where the student body is 65 percent female. An annual freshman icebreaker called "Dickerella," in which women and men pair off for trips to a local burger joint named Dick's, has become a farce: "A lot of the guys have two dates," says Sarah Johnson, a senior.

Nor are they at Concordia College in St. Paul, Minn., which is 61 percent female. "If I'm about five minutes late for a class, when I walk in and look up, at least three quarters of the seats in my class are filled with girls," says junior Chad Nelson.

In short, they're not there across the country. This year, women are expected to earn just over 57 percent of all bachelor's degrees, compared with 43 percent in 1970 and under 24 percent in 1950. The U.S. Department of Education now projects that by 2008 women will outnumber men in undergraduate and graduate programs by 9.2 million to 6.9 million. The trend is moving quickly; if it continues at this pace, "the graduation line in the year 2068 will be all females," says Tom Mortenson, a higher-education policy analyst.

Armed with better grades, better résumés, and a clearer sense of future goals, many females reach the senior year of high school primed for the college admissions game. Males, meanwhile, are tempted by fast cash in a boom-time economy, preferring $30,000 starting salaries in such fields as air-conditioner maintenance and Web design to four years of *Beowulf* and student loans.

The growing split in post-secondary paths might do more to foster gender equality than any constitutional amendment or court decision. With an edge in education, women could close the salary gap and increasingly move into positions of power — as heads of corporations, presidents of universities, and political leaders.

But that's assuming higher education remains the key to upward mobility — a big "if," warn some, who foresee a time not too distant when degrees are not so prized, and skipping college might be a wiser career choice.

Past parity. Since women stepped into the majority on campuses in 1979, the college gender gap has widened at virtually every type of school: large and small, public and private, two-year and four-year. From the 23,617-student, state-run University of New Mexico (57 percent female) to 2,032-student, Catholic-affiliated Edgewood College in Wisconsin (73 percent female) to the mammoth University of California system (seven of the eight campuses have female majorities), women are flooding colleges and universities.

And where are the boys?

Logan Sieg, a 17-year-old senior at Gettysburg Area High School in Gettysburg, Pa., will be picking up his diploma this June. Come September, though, he won't be on a college campus. "I have enough money in the bank, and college would be a snap" he says. "But I have a car to pay for." Instead of pursuing a bachelor's degree, he plans on learning air-conditioner and heating system repair at a local technical institute; a friend's brother, a graduate of the trade school, made $10 an hour his first year out, plus generous overtime. While Sieg sees the value of high school math — "you need to know the volume of rooms, the circulation" — he says that other intellectual pursuits have little bearing on his career plans. "In academic English, all the teacher talks about is college prep, college prep" he moans. "I raise my hand: 'I'm not going to college, I'm going to technical school."

With unemployment at its lowest point in a generation, it's not surprising that some kids pass up four more years of classes. "It's easier to go out and get a job now than to do the hard work and stay in college," says Claudia Goldin, an economic historian at Harvard University. "For lots of people it's 'buy now, think later'" — a mind-set that can have severe consequences. Male college graduates earn, on average, over $23,000 a year more than men who have only high school diplomas, and that income disparity is growing. Nevertheless, boys are leading the charge into the workplace — they account for 57 percent of those ages 16 to 24 in the labor force who hold only a high school diploma.

Where the boys are. "I know a *lot* of guys from my hometown who quit college to run their own store, or to have a Schwan's [food delivery] route, or to do some of these jobs where, for their age, they're getting paid really well" says Shawn Vogt, a junior at Hamline University's College of Liberal Arts in St. Paul. "That may not be the case once we all graduate from college . . . but at this point, they have high-paying jobs. And I don't know of any women in those positions."

A real growth industry for young men subscribing to the "less learning, more earning" credo is computers, where pay is high and the future bright. "If making money is your first goal, and if you are competent in high-paying skills, there's no reason to finish your degree," says Stephen Trachtenberg, president of George Washington

University in Washington, D.C. "We shouldn't be surprised by that. It's demonstrated to us on a regular basis by people who sign up with the NBA [National Basketball Association] or [by] baseball players." His son, a 1997 graduate of Columbia University, had a roommate who dropped out during his sophomore year to take a computer-related job. "By the time my son got his B.A., his former roommate was making $100,000 a year," says Trachtenberg.

Michael Rahimpour, 23, knows all about the fast money to be made in computers. The San Diego native has been designing Web sites since 1993. After bouncing around a few junior colleges, he dropped out after realizing that "the best education is given by corporations these days." He adds that "pretty much everyone I know is taking the route of not finishing college — it's just too attractive." It certainly is in Rahimpour's case: He pulls down $76,500 a year in base salary as the webmaster for PalmPilot-maker 3Com.

Computer companies are so desperate to snag fresh talent that many are actively recruiting high school seniors. Cisco Systems, for example, runs two-year classes in high schools that certify graduates to become network administrators. And Intel travels far and wide to snatch up workers for its chip-making plants; in Oregon, Portland-based recruiters often journey 217 miles southwest to Marshfield High School in Coos Bay to entice students to put off college in favor of a high-tech factory. Most of the workers Intel walks away with are boys; Walt Biddle, executive director of the Career Training Foundation, a nonprofit group that supports U.S. trade schools, estimates that two thirds of the people entering the information-technology industry are male.

Girls, meanwhile, are busy making themselves into strong candidates for admission to college. "They mature sooner, so they get more serious about their schoolwork," says Delsie Phillips, director of admissions at Haverford College in Haverford, Pa., echoing a near-unanimous sentiment among college officials. "It really shows up when you start reading applications. Girls have followed through and done all the things they are supposed to do, while boys are still trying to find themselves." Though girls do slightly worse than boys on standardized tests — in 1998, their mean score on the SAT was 7 points lower on the verbal section and 35 points lower on math — admissions officials say grades, class rank, and activities are given far more weight. Slightly outnumbered in the overall population of 15-to-19-year-olds, girls graduate from high school at a higher rate than boys; in 1996, 51.2 percent of high school graduates were female. Girls accounted for 53.5 percent of SAT takers that year, and 69.7 percent of female graduates enrolled in college within a year of graduating, compared with only 60.1 percent of boys.

Clearly, part of the trend in college enrollment stems from advances in society that have given women more choices. They are no longer expected to take the homemaker route or to matriculate solely for the purpose of earning their "M.R.S. degree": that is, a husband. "When I was a high school counselor 20 years ago, I had many parents say, 'I want my daughter to take home economics because she's just going to get married,'" says Nancy Perry, executive director of the American School Counselor Association. "Women believe they can achieve now, and they go for it."

This also brings a large number of older women to campus, especially to state universities that cater to "nontraditional" students. "A lot [of women] put off finishing college to follow a husband or because of families," says Michael O'Connor, director of enrollment services at Old Dominion University in Norfolk, Va., which is 56 percent female. "Now they're re-entering the work force, and they need to be retained."

A small pool. A particularly large gender gap among African-Americans, who make up about 11 percent of the nation's undergraduate population, also contributes to the skew. Nearly 63 percent of African-American undergraduates are women, and of the nation's 117 historically black colleges and universities, only one — all-male Morehouse College in Atlanta — has a majority of men. High dropout and incarceration rates are to blame for the discrepancy: In 1994, there were more African-American males in jail or prison than enrolled in college. "You've got fewer and fewer black males who are eligible for college," says Anthony Jones, director of admissions at Fisk University in Nashville, which is 71 percent female. "Then you have to find ones who meet Fisk's criteria, and it's a bit selective. We end up having to recruit from a very small pool."

But girls in general seem steps ahead long before college appears on the radar. As early as fourth grade, according to a Department of Education survey, they spend more time on homework than boys do, and they are less likely to zone out in front of the television for hours on end. More girls become high school newspaper editors, honor society members, and community service volunteers.

Male peer pressure, which often includes a strong anti-intellectual component, may also contribute to the trend. "I raised a boy, and I'm aware of the degree to which acting enthusiastic in your studies is not something that boys are encouraged to do." says Margaret Miller, president of the American Association for Higher Education (AAHE). "Being good in school is associated with femininity."

Some believe that educators on the elementary and secondary levels are not helping matters by fostering a bias toward girls. They argue that the tendency of boys to be rambunctious, to ignore directions, and to produce sloppy assignments draws the ire of teachers who prefer more well-behaved, manageable girls. Perry of the counselors' association agrees that young girls may do better in part because "they are more willing to comply with their teachers than boys; their papers are neater."

It is a theory that flies in the face of conventional wisdom, which for years has depicted classrooms as chilly places for girls. Judith Kleinfeld, a professor of psychology at the University of Alaska-Fairbanks, attacked that viewpoint in a controversial paper last year, in which she concluded: "Males are . . . more apt than females to believe that the school climate is hostile to them, that teachers do not expect as much from them and give them less encouragement to do their best."

"It really begins early," says Mortenson. "The boys tend to be less focused." It is a "learning style" that can give teachers — 70 percent of whom are female — fits. A disproportionate number of boys end up in special education — they account for over three quarters of the enrollment in programs for those with behavioral or developmental disorders. Boys also fail to finish high school at a far higher rate; between October 1995 and October 1996, they accounted for 58 percent of the nation's dropouts.

The new dating game. With boys a rarer on-campus sight, college social life has taken a new turn. A joke that makes the rounds at Seattle Pacific goes, "What's the difference between an SPU woman and a trash can? A trash can gets taken out once a week." At UNC-Chapel Hill, one recent alumna says, "The women develop eating disorders, and the men develop huge egos." Sorority sisters at UNC often outnumber fraternity brothers by 3 to 1 at Greek system parties. "The guys here notice that they're outnumbered, and they take advantage of it," says Meredith Gayle, a junior. "They date more girls, sometimes several at a time. They can get away with it." The men, by contrast, rarely complain about their minority status. "The ratio was a determinant in my coming here," says Matthew Carroll, another junior. "You can always go on a date if you want to. It's just a matter of having the time and a car."

This is not to say that a school dominated by women is necessarily an unpleasant place to be. Lauren Burns, a junior at UNC, says, "I wouldn't change the fact that there are so many females. We really feel a bond. It makes more women speak up; we're not afraid."

On the whole, though, administrators are concerned that students are missing out on a well-rounded experience. "College is for a lot more than going to class," says Phillips of Haverford, a men's college until 1980 that is now 52 percent female. "There's all kind of interactions that take place, intellectual and social in nature, and male and female point of view are important, just like viewpoints from different nationalities and different ethnic groups."

In an effort to bolster male enrollments, some colleges are putting greater emphasis on sports, an area in which men are thought to have a disproportionate interest. "We did win the Sun Bowl and win in our conference," says Sandra Ware, dean of admissions at Texas Christian University (59 percent female) in Fort Worth, lauding the school's champion football team. "So we're hoping that [males] were watching and paying attention to that." The University of Dallas (56 percent female) went so far as to form a varsity baseball squad, which added 28 much-sought-after men to the school in 1997. And as part of a five-year plan to attract more males, Fisk is contemplating a move from the National Collegiate Athletic Association's Division III up to the more competitive Division II.

Other schools have fiddled with their recruitment materials, redesigning catalogs and revamping direct-mail campaigns. Edgewood is considering packaging their view books in different envelopes, depending on the sex of the recipient. "We're taking a cue from

Bon Appetit magazine, which tried to increase their male readership with different color schemes and graphics," says Scott Flanagan, Edgewood's dean of admissions and financial aid. In 1997, Whitman College (55 percent female) in Walla Walla, Wash., sent a second mailing of recruitment materials to 5,900 men — but not to women. The move gained the school 40 more male applicants.

Male preference? Schools say they stop short of offering "affirmative action for men," but some confide that giving male applicants a slight break is becoming a standard, albeit unspoken, practice. "Colleges and universities are dipping down deeper into their male pool than their female pool," says AAHE president Miller. "It's definitely out there," agrees Joan Mudge, director of college counseling at the all-girls Garrison Forest School in Owings Mills, Md. "They don't come right out and say they're discriminating against our girls, but they are." When calling schools to inquire why highly qualified female applicants were rejected, Mudge says admissions directors will "hedge and hedge before saying, 'Our female applicant pool was just incredible this year.'"

Such griping must seem ironic to many women who remember when higher education, especially at four-year schools, was a privilege reserved mostly for their brothers. Indeed, the gender flip-flop could be viewed as an amazing success story. But some observers who study the gender patterns of the work force warn that the picture is not as rosy as it might appear. Among the population of full-time workers, women with bachelor's degrees still make only $4,708 more on average than men holding nothing more than a high school diploma; that's close to $20,000 less than the college-degree premium enjoyed by men. And there are concerns that most areas of study preferred by women — English over engineering, psychology over computer science — are reinforcing their secondary position in the economy. "Every sort of job that's associated with females is also associated with declining status," says Barbara Miller, an anthropologist and former director of women's studies at George Washington. "They're less economically promising in terms of lifetime earnings."

"We still find that women are more likely to be concentrated in female fields, which have lower pay, fewer opportunities for advancement, and less prestige," says Judith Sturnick, director of the American Council on Education's Office of Women in Higher Education. In part this stems from choices that are almost as much about lifestyle as they are about ambition: "A typical high school male student may feel he has to go directly into an engineering or business track right away," says Edgewood's Flanagan. (Indeed, schools with strong engineering programs — like large state schools — have not experienced this trend as dramatically.) "Female students have a much more enlightened view that, to succeed latter in life, they need an education with more breadth to it."

But Sturnick cites the current rise of corporate-sponsored schools — such as the Cisco computer-networking program — which train mostly men for high-paying, often technology-related jobs, as women slog along at traditional colleges. "Will we set up a separate track for education which will primarily benefit men, which will allow them to enter the job market with higher pay at a higher salary," Sturnick asks, "while women continue on the baccalaureate track, end up debt laden, and then wind up three or four years behind in a profession?" She says higher education could become devalued because of its increasing feminization — the same phenomenon that has occurred with elementary school teachers — and that earning a bachelor's degree will someday be considered a foolhardy economic decision. "When there begins to be a predominance of female members in any area, the value of that area goes down," she says. "Is it possible we are devaluing higher education? There's a potential for that as more and more women dominate in degree achievement."

The still-small number of women majoring in math and the sciences also has some education watchers troubled. Though many traditionally "male" majors — like business — have moved toward parity or are now female dominated, women are still vastly outnumbered on campuses with strong engineering and physical-sciences programs. The student body at the California Institute of Technology, for example, is still 73 percent male. "What we're seeing now is that there is a tremendous gap in computer science," says Sandy Bernard, president of the American Association of University Women. "That one will be really significant." She worries that women's lack of those types of degrees will sentence them to also-ran status in the high-tech workplace, where the big money will be.

Social distortion. Tom Mortenson foresees another problem, one with major implications for the American way of courtship, marriage, and family life. "If the educational attainment differences continue to grow at the rate they are, a shrinking number of college-educated women are going to find college-educated men to marry," he cautions. It's a trend that is already familiar to African-American women, many of whom bemoan the fact that there are relatively few college-educated black men to choose from.

Occasional griping about dim romantic prospects aside, most female students realize how far they've come. "You know, 20 years ago it was not this way at all," says Jen Balk, a Hamline sophomore. "It was all the men going to school and getting the good jobs, and there was such a barrier. Now that we have the opportunity, everybody's taking it." And what of the men who are increasingly not part of that "everybody"? If college degrees remain an entree to wealth and status in the 21st century, males may have to get used to the same second-class status that American women so long endured, as highly educated females become the majority among the nation's intellectual, economic, and even power elite. "I hope the men can accommodate what's going to happen," says Mortenson, "when the woman becomes the main breadwinner in the family." It could prove enough of a shock to send the guys scurrying off to hit the books — and fill out some college applications.

THE ART OF GIVING

A. A. Milne

English Humorist, the originator of the immensely popular stories of Christopher Robin and his toy bear, Winnie-the-Pooh.

Works: *Winnie - the - Pooh* (1926). *The Hours at Pooh Corner* (1928)

Very few women understand the art of giving presents. They say to themselves: "What does Archie want? He smokes, doesn't he? What does he smoke? John Cotton? Then let us give him a pound of John Cotton." Now that is a silly present, because, if Archie smokes John Cotton, he has been buying John Cotton for years; which proves that he is well able to buy yet one more pound of John Cotton for himself. It is useless to give a man a present which he can buy for himself; you are giving him no more than a twenty-five shilling postal order. The art of giving men presents is to give them something which they cannot buy for themselves: something which, without your co-operation, they would never be able to possess.

Let us look at this question frankly. What is the average man's position in the home? What is he doing there at all? Observe this small but well-appointed house. If we open the door, what do we find inside? We find one wife, one cook, one house-parlourmaid, one nurse, and one girl-baby. Five females, and all as happy as happy together. Why are they so happy? Because somewhere, in another part of the town, there is a man earning money. And is not the man also happy? Certainly he is. Why? Because all these five females are spending his money in the way which will give him most happiness. Bless them!

The fact is, then, that man has a genius for making money, and woman has a genius for spending it. This fact should always be remembered when Christmas comes round. It is foolish for women to say: "My husband (uncle, brother, father, cousin) is a poor earner; what can I give him?" The thing to say is: "My husband (father, brother, cousin, uncle) is a hopeless shopper; what can I, with my genius for shopping, buy for him?"

Now this is where all the comic papers, which make their annual fun of a wife's presents to her husband, seem to me to be absurdly wrong. A woman gives a box of high-coloured Cabajos to a husband who smokes Coronas, and is ridiculed by the Press for it. How unimaginative! That woman knows much more about the art of present-giving than does the Corona-buying wife. She understands that to give a Corona to a man who is long-practised in the art of buying Coronas is to give him no surprise, no thrill, no pleasure, but to give him a Ćabajo, which he is physically unable to demand himself at a tobacconist's, is, at any rate, to bring something new into his life. And who knows? He may for years have wanted Cabajos for his friends; or, if not for his friends, for people like policemen on whom, it is assumed, a better brand would be wasted. How many times have we men said nervously to each other, looking sidelong at some third party: "I wonder if he expects a tip?" and how often we have felt that the difficulty would be resolved, could we but offer him a Cabajo from our well-fitted case, with the friendly, if slightly misleading, phrase, "Have a cigar?"

Consider also this other stale property of the comic draughtsman — the highly coloured tie. What a dull present to the City-going husband would be one of those dear old black ties which he has always bought for himself, and always worn, this twenty years past! And what a thrilling present the purple and scarlet effect which you are knitting for him! More than women realize do men long for a little romance, a little colour in their lives. Could old Brown, that steady-going gentleman, buy a purple and scarlet cravat for himself? Never! The stares, the ridicule! But if he can say, "Well, you see, my wife made it for me, and I don't like to hurt her feelings," how splendid is his position! He foots it down Cheapside feeling himself a toreador and a blessed martyr all in one.

But there is another type of present which a woman may well give a man; something which, in theory, he is able to buy for himself, but, in practice, never does buy. The most obvious examples are found among the jewelled decorations which, as unobtrusively as possible, he wears about his person. No man ever bought anything but the plainest rolled-gold studs and links for himself; the woman who can afford it may step forward with her mother-of-pearl and enamel. Another good example is the walking-stick or the umbrella. One cannot have too many of these, nor too beautiful. And if I am getting beyond the reach of your purse, let me put in a word for the homely braces. Probably no woman has ever considered seriously the startling fact that not one man in ten of her acquaintance has a spare pair of braces. There is a mysterious something, I know not what, which seems to prohibit a man from buying a second pair, so firmly does he trust to the pair in use. Yet a reserve pair, presented by some friend, would not only be useful, but would lift him so high in his own esteem above his acquaintance, that he would feel the whole world to be at his feet. Forgive me for touching upon this delicate subject, but blue is the best colour, and they are quite cheap.

Next we approach the matter of golf balls. This may be a personal idiosyncrasy, but I hold that a box of golf balls is almost the best present of all. But, you will say, are you not always buying golf balls for yourself? Always. But never in boxes. A man buys golf balls in the professional's shop on his way to the first tee; he puts a couple in his pocket. How could he buy a box then? Yet no golfer, I think, but longed to have a box of his own, over which he could gloat lovingly, telling himself that this or that one would be the first to do the long seventh in three.

Almost the best present, I said. For the best present of all is books. I speak not only as a writer whose books are waiting in the best shops to catch the eye of the generous giver, but also as a lay-reader who can never have too many books given to him. There is no pleasure to equal the pleasure of opening a parcel of books; to buy them for oneself is to lose all the wonder and half the thrill. "But how shall I know what books he likes?" you ask. "Madam," I answer modestly, "is it for me to — er — " and then I look on the ground, and cough a little, wondering privately what the woman is making such a fuss about. "Oh, but he's read all yours," she says quickly. "I mean, what others?" Then let me suggest, madam, that you give him the books which you think you will like.

This has two advantages. For, first, you can read them through quickly before you send them off to him, thus getting them practically for nothing; and, secondly, you can find out in this way if the fellow is really worth any consideration at all. There are books which a kindred soul must like, or lose for ever his claim to kinship. As soon as you have read them, you will know, and by that shall you test his claim. Does he applaud them enthusiastically, then you shall marry him; or, being already married, shall visit him; or, calling yourself his aunt, shall address him still as "Dearest nephew." But if he neglect to read them, or, reading them, dismiss them with a "Not bad," then shall you jilt him, cut him, disinherit him. And next Christmas you shall buy two boxes of cigars, one Coronas, one Cabajos. And you shall take the labels off the Coronas and put them upon the Cabajos for him. And, being a snob, as is now obvious, he will smoke them all, to the bitter end, the oh! so bitter end, thinking them Coronas. And the other box you shall send to me, if you like, for having warned you.

Sex as Symbol in Fashion Advertising and Analyzing Signs and Sign Systems

Arthur Asa Berger

Professor of Broadcast Communication Arts at San Francisco State University. His work on popular culture includes *The Comic Stripped American, The TV-Guided American*, and *Television as an Instrument of Terror*. Throughout his career, Berger has attempted to make accessible the language of media analysis and cultural critique.

Sex as Symbol in Fashion Advertising

While reading an issue of *Vogue* recently, I noticed that I was, somehow, taken by a number of the advertisements for fashions and cosmetics. Many of these advertisements contained striking photographs and suggestive (and in some cases rather overt) copy. I found myself absorbed by the advertisements. They had a remarkable power over me — to seize my attention and to stimulate, if only for a moment, fantasies of an erotic nature. It was not only the physical characteristics of the models that affected me; rather it was a kind of gestalt effect. There was the element of graphic design, of color, of light, and a host of other matters that "conspired" to excite me.

"What's going on?" I asked myself. That question led me to consider how magazine advertising works to stimulate desire and sell clothes, cosmetics, and everything else that is connected with beauty (in this case) or any product.

In analyzing an advertisement there are a number of factors that we must consider, such as the ambience, the design, the use of white space, the significant images and symbols, the use of language, the type faces used, and the item itself (and its role and function in society). We can also consider how the advertisement attempts to "sell" us and what roles it offers us to imitate, as well as examine how social phenomena might be reflected, indirectly. (Here I'm thinking about such things as alienation, boredom, conformism, generational conflict, and so on.) We can use whatever concepts we have at our command from history, psychology, sociology, anthropology, and any other disciplines to help us "dissect" the advertisement. In applying all of the above it is important to keep one cardinal principle in mind: The creators of any advertisement are trying to generate some kind of an effect or emotional response. So we must start with the effect and work backwards. What is the fantasy? And how is it induced?

SELLING MAGIC

I will answer these questions by examining some of the

advertisements in the April 1978 issue of *Vogue* magazine. I've selected advertisements that, for some reason, caught my attention for a moment and that I think are interesting and worth examining closely.

Let me start with a double-page advertisement by Revlon for its Formula 2 cleanser and moisturizer. The left-hand page of the advertisement is devoted to an extreme close-up of a woman's face, but the face is rendered by using quarter-inch squares of various colors. We are, in fact, given an optical illusion. If we squint, or place the magazine fifteen feet away from us, the squares merge together and form a face. But at arm's length, the face is somewhat distorted and out of focus. It is also larger than life in size. From there we move over to the right-hand page, which has a great deal of white space and is formally designed, approximating axial balance. Generally speaking, large amounts of white space and axial balance (and formality) are associated with quality and "class" in most people's mind.

The copy of the ad stresses science and technology as opposed to nature. We find the following suggestive words and phrases in the advertisement:

Revlon Research Group
skincare system
natural electricity
formula
skincare that's simple, scientific

precision tip
beauty technology
hygiene
principle

All of these terms are signifiers for science and technology; we are led to think of scientists in laboratories discovering remarkable things that lead to "the New-Face Hygiene" and "beautiful life for your skin." A smaller photograph on this page shows two medicinal-looking bottles, in which the future-age Formula 2 cleanser and moisturizer are packaged.

Though this is something of a generalization, there seems to be a polar opposition in the public's mind that posits a world divided between culture (and with it science and technology) and nature. Thus the people who created the Revlon advertisement had two possibilities: to stress nature and all that's suggested by it, or to stress culture, in this case, science and technology. They chose the latter course and offered their readers a minicourse in science and technology: *This* principle leads to *those* results.

Ultimately what is being sold here — and what is being sold in most cosmetics ads — is magic, and that is where the large rendering of the woman's face comes in. It is an optical illusion that has two functions: First, it catches our attention because when we look at the face we see that it is really only a huge patchwork of squares. At first glance it seems out of focus and strange. But, if we squint or stare at it, magically it becomes a face, just the same way that Revlon Formula 2's "beauty technology of the future" gives you the gift of "life" (for your skin). Just as the law of closure forces us to complete that which is unfinished, we find ourselves obliged to make sense of the picture, and we visualize the woman's face even more completely than we find it. This act of visualization is what is asked of patrons or purchasers of the product. From the bits and pieces of their old faces they are asked (almost forced) to envision the new faces they will have with Formula 2.

Now that the face is taken care of, let us "finish off" the job (the law of closure once again) and take care of the entire body. For this we can use Benandré, which says it "will do for your body what a facial does for your face." This single-page advertisement has, like the Revlon advertisement, axial balance and a considerable amount of white space. It shows a woman in a glass bathtub bathing herself in "Mediterranean blue" water. A bit of greenery signifies the Mediterranean here. The woman's face is cleary shown, in profile, but her body is not. We see only a diffused figure in blue-green water. Benandré promises that its special form of collagen (a protein contained in the connective tissues and bones, which yields gelatin on boiling) helps the body retain moisture and helps it to restore moisture it loses during the day.

This matter of keeping the skin (and body) moist is interesting. A great deal of cosmetic advertising stresses wetness, moisture, and related concepts, as if the body were in danger of becoming an arid desert, devoid of life, dry, uninteresting, and infertile. These ads suggest that women fear, or should fear, losing their body fluids, which becomes the equivalent of losing their capacity to reproduce. This, in turn, is connected with sexuality and desirability. Anxiety over the body as a kind of wasteland is implicit in appeals in advertisements about retaining and restoring moisture. Dehydration is a metaphor for loss of sexual attractiveness and capacity, that is, desexualization.

Dry skin becomes, then, a sign of a woman who is all dried up and who is not sexually responsive — and who may also be sterile. This is because water is connected, in our psyches, with birth. It is also tied to purity, as in baptismal rites when sin is cleansed from a person. All of this suggests that words and images that picture a body of a woman as being dehydrated and losing water have great resonance.

In *Man and His Symbols*, Carl Jung (1968: 29) writes:

> Every concept in our conscious mind, in short, has its own psychic associations. While such associations may vary in intensity . . . they are capable of changing the "normal" character of that concept. It may even become something quite different as it drifts below the level of consciousness.
>
> These subliminal aspects of everything that happens to us may seem to play very little part in our daily lives. But in dream analysis, where the psychologist is dealing with expressions of the unconscious, they are very relevant, for they are the almost invisible roots of our conscious thoughts. That is why commonplace objects or ideas can assume such powerful psychic significance in a dream.

If we substitute "advertisements" for "dreams" in the above quotation, we can understand why and how we are affected so profoundly by images and words.

The copy in the Benandré ad is full of purple prose indicating power and luxury. Some of the more interesting words and phrases appear below:

lavished
unique
expensive
luxury
rare oils
prefer
enriching
treat yourself
beneficial
beauty treatment

This product is sold as a kind of indulgence for women. The copy hints at sex ("You'll make the skin of your body as nice to touch as the skin on your face. Just ask the one who touches you most."), which is always a strong selling point for beauty aids. But the pictorial element is connected with symbols of innocence —baptism, cleanliness, and so on. And the towel in the lower right-hand corner of the ad is a chaste white. From a psychoanalytic perspective, there is also something regressive about all this. It is almost as if the woman emerges with the skin of a baby. She also is quite undefined sexually; we are certain we are seeing a woman, but her sexuality has been subdued a great deal, which is in keeping with "class" as we have been taught to think of it.

Next let us move on to some clothes for our moist and soft-skinned beauty: Danskins. The advertisement for Danskins shows three female bodies lying down on a blue-green piece of fabric that may also be water — it is hard to say. What is interesting is the arrangement of the bodies, all horizontal and jammed together. Two of the models are lying with their heads on the left and the third is between them with her head to the right side of the picture. Although they touch one another, each seems unaware of any of the others — they all stare off into space in separate directions.

The Danskin ad is extremely simple and formal. It has three elements: a headline, the photograph of the three women, and an element containing six lines of copy, all in capitals. The product advertised is a "freestyle" leotard/swimsuit that comes in various "sensuous styles and colors." The large element of white space contrasts with the crowding in the photograph, a crowding that a Marxist would say reflects a diffuse alienation among the women, who are touching one another but do not seem to be aware of each other. They are all, we must assume, pursuing their private fantasies.

Finally, let us move on to an ad depicting a fully dressed woman in Calvin Klein separates. Here we find a model with her right hand on her hip, her left hand behind her head, and her left knee bent (in the "bashful knee pose") and prominently displayed. The background is gray and there is hardly any text. The shirt the model wears has a plunging neckline, but there is no cleavage showing, and there is a slit in the skirt, which enables her to display her knee.

We are given little textual information: the designer, Calvin Klein; the store where the outfit can be purchased, I. Magnin; and the fabric manufacturer, the Ideacomo group.

The model has long, curly hair. She has a rather cold look on her face, a look that is commonly seen in high-fashion advertising. And she is posed in a way that emphasizes her arms and legs rather than her breasts and hips. Thus attention is focused on her appendages, which are sexually undifferentiated. Yet there is something of a sexually alluring quality about this pose, which shows a lot of upper leg. It may have something to do with the tilt of the hips, the twist of the torso, and the neckline. Perhaps the unnaturalness of the pose is important, also.

BREAKING THE ADVERTISING CODE

The codes of simplicity, white space and formality, appear in the Calvin Klein advertisement just as they did in all the other advertisements discussed to this point. These "couture" codes are learned by people, who are taught, by advertisers, to associate simplicity, spaciousness, and formal structure with "class." In the same manner, we are taught the "meanings" of various typefaces and kinds of images. Soft focus signifies dream-like states, formal structure or design implies "classic" (whatever that means), and so on. All of these associations are carried around in our heads, so that all the advertiser has to do is "activate" us by striking the appropriate responsive chord. As Tony Schwartz (1974: 24-25) writes in *The Responsive Chord:*

> The critical task is to design our package of stimuli so that it resonates with information already stored with the individual and thereby induces the desired learning or behavioral effect. Resonance takes place when the stimuli put into our communication evoke *meaning* in a listener or viewer. That which we put into the communication has no meaning in itself. The meaning of our communication is what a listener or viewer *gets out* of his experience with the communicator's stimulus.

Culture, and "couture," which is part of culture, is a collection of codes we learn that provide us with meaning in the world. But how, specifically, do these codes work, and how do we find meaning in advertisements (as well as other forms of communication)?

In a magazine (or other form of print) advertisement there are two ways that information is communicated — through the text and through pictorial and design elements. We can examine the text to determine what appeals are being pressed forward and what means are used to lead the reader/viewer to desire the product. Anxiety may be provoked. There may be inducements to self-gratifications of varying natures. Snobbery may be invoked. Any number of techniques of persuasion can be used here. And in the pictorial material there is also a "language" that may be employed to generate the desired feelings and fantasies. I have mentioned some of these techniques: design, size, color, grain, focus, and so on. And I have suggested that we learn to associate certain kinds of advertisements with certain kinds of fashions.

Can we take matters a step further? Can we explain how these associations are made and how the various signs and symbols generate the meanings they do? In some cases, yes. To do so we must expand our vocabulary of analysis. I would like to reintroduce some terms from semiology at this point:

metaphor: relationship by analogy (example: my love is a red rose)
metonymy: relationship by association (example: rich people and mansions)
icon: relationship by resemblance (example: photograph of an object)
index: relationship by implication (example: smoke implies fire)
symbol: relationship by convention (example: Star of David and Jews)

There is a problem in differentiating between metonymy and symbol that I find hard to solve. Neither are motivated or natural, but relationships by association seem to be stronger than relationships by convention. Anything can be a symbol once people learn to accept it as such. But the association between wealth and large mansions seems quite logical. Wealthy people, people with "class," tend to live in large houses, have a great deal of land and space for themselves, and are powerful. Thus spatiality becomes associated with wealth and class indirectly, through the matter of living space found in large homes.

In metonymy, then, the relationships are stronger than in symbols. One important form of metonymy is synecdoche, in which a part stands for a whole or vice versa. Monoca (1977: 135) in *How to*

Read a Film suggests that in film "close shots of marching feet to represent an army" is synecdochic and "failing calendar pages" to indicate the passing of time are metonymic, and that it is through metonymy and synecdoche that Hollywood and films in general are able to communicate with people so quickly and powerfully. Thus, for example, sweat is an index of body heat (or nervous anxiety) that functions metonymically since "associated details invoke an abstract idea."

Magazine advertisements function in much the same way, using whatever devices they can to signify "abstract ideas" — what we call signifieds — such as passion, love, romance, and so on. Because these advertisements can use language, they can use metaphor, but more often they also wish to imply or suggest things (fantasies of exotic love, hopes for beauty) through pictorial elements that make use of the devices described above in various combinations.

With these terms we can do more than simply say that signs and symbols work on the basis of associations that people learn and that become codes by which they interpret the world and function in it. For example, let us consider our first advertisement, the one for Revlon's Formula 2 cleanser and moisturizer. Although there are many things going on in this advertisement it seems to me that the most important thing in the ad is the way it forces the reader to turn the optical illusion into a face, which suggests, perhaps subliminally, *magic*. Most cosmetic advertisements involve a belief in magic, but usually the appeals are verbal. In this advertisement, however, we are forced to do a great deal of work, work that "convinces" us that it is logical to believe in magic. Why not? We've just done something magical. We've seen that magic works, with our own eyes.

I see this process as indexical. The Revlon products promise beauty by magic just the way the square patches hold the promise of a face, once we learn how to see the patches correctly. The implication is that Revlon is magic and it will work for you the way your eyes work to figure out the optical illusion. There may also be an element of suggesting that beauty is an illusion and is attainable by all who can employ the correct magic. The picture of the woman in the ad is indexical, but the bottles are symbolic and rely upon the conventional look of medicinal products for their power. The stylishness of the advertisement, with its use of white space and simplicity, is also symbolic. There is nothing natural or logical about our associating white space and simplicity with "class." It is historical, part of our culture, and something that most of us learn.

In the Revlon advertisement and in all advertisements we find a kind of chain reaction taking place. The verbal and pictorial elements in the advertisement function as signifiers that generate feelings and beliefs or signifieds for those who look at and read the advertisement. These feelings and beliefs (and, we might add, hopes, fantasies, and the like) are based on codes (structured belief systems), which, in turn, operate via metaphor, metonymy, icon, index, and symbols in various combinations. Thus, in order to determine how advertisements and other forms of visual-verbal communication generate meaning, we can move beyond the notion of codes and see how the codes themselves function.

It is a fascinating business taking advertisements apart to see how they function and determining what they reflect about society. It is also a perilous business, for there is always the possibility that we are not examining society's fantasies, or those of the creators of the advertisements, but our own. In *The Strategy of Desire*, Ernest Dichter (1960: 11), one of the founding fathers of motivation research, writes:

> Human desire is the raw material we are working with. The strategy of desire is the tool of shaping the human factor, the most important aspect of our worldly arsenal. Human progress is a conquest of the animal within us. No conquest is possible without strategy.

Whether or not advertising and other tools of persuasion are leading us to higher levels of development is questionable. One thing seems quite evident — knowing the strategies used by the people who work at creating and shaping our desire is important, for then we can make more rational decisions and avoid manipulation. The person who is a slave to fashion is often also a slave to his or her own emotions — emotions that can be manipulated by the fashion advertising industry. But escape is possible.

Analyzing Signs and Sign Systems

I would like to offer a check-list for analyzing photographs, advertisements, and frames from films in addition to less complicated signs. I am concerned with the various kinds of signs being used, how they generate meaning, how they relate to one another, what they reflect about our society and culture, and the problems they pose for the semiologist or other "interpreters" of signs.

Let us assume we are dealing with an advertisement in a magazine. We should be concerned with some or all of the following matters:

A. What is the general ambience of the advertisement? What mood does it create? How does it do this?

B. What is the design of the advertisement? Does it use axial balance or some other form? How are the basic components or elements of the advertisement arranged?

C. What is the relationship that exists between pictorial elements and written material and what does this tell us?

D. What is the spatiality in the advertisement? Is there a lot of "white space" or is the advertisement full of graphic and written elements (that is, "busy")?

E. What signs and symbols do we find? What role do the various signs and symbols play in the advertisement?

F. If there are figures (men, women, children, animals) in the advertisement, what are they like? What can be said about their facial expressions, poses, hairstyle, age, sex, hair color, ethnicity, education, occupation, relationships (of one to the other), and so on?

G. What does the background tell us? Where is the action in the advertisement taking place and what significance does this background have?

H. What action is taking place in the advertisement and what significance does this action have? (This might be described as the plot of the advertisement.)

I. What theme or themes do we find in the advertisement? What is the advertisement about? (The plot of an advertisement may involve a man and a woman drinking but the theme might be jealousy, faithlessness, ambition, passion, etc.)

J. What about the language used in the advertisement? Does it essentially provide information or generate some kind of an emotional response? Or both? What techniques are used by the copywriter: humor, alliteration, "definitions" of life, comparisons, sexual innuendo, and so on?

K. What typefaces are used and what impressions do these typefaces convey?

L. What is the item being advertised and what role does it play in American culture and society?

M. What about aesthetic decisions? If the advertisement is a photograph, what kind of a shot is it? What significance do long shots, medium shots, close-ups have? What about the lighting, use of color, angle of the shot?

N. What sociological, political, economic or cultural attitudes are indirectly reflected in the advertisement? An advertisement may be about a pair of blue jeans but it might, indirectly, reflect such matters as sexism, alienation, stereotyped thinking, conformism, generational conflict, loneliness, elitism, and so on.

THE MYTH OF THE MATRIARCH

Gloria Naylor (1950-)

African-American Writer. Began to write novels after reading Toni Morrison's *The Bluest Eye*. Her work reflects a moral and spiritual sensibility. Novels: *The Women of Brewster Place* (1982), *Linden Hills* (1985), *Mama Day* (1988), *Bailey's Cafe* (1992), *The Men of Brewster Place* (1998).

The strong black woman. All my life I've seen her. In books she is Faulkner's impervious Dilsey, using her huge dark arms to hold together the crumbling spirits and household of the Compsons. In the movies she is the quintessential Mammy, chasing after Scarlett O'Hara with forgotten sunbonnets and shrill tongue-lashings about etiquette. On television she is Sapphire of *Amos 'n' Andy* or a dozen variations of her — henpecking black men, herding white children, protecting her brood from the onslaughts of the world. She is the supreme matriarch — alone, self-sufficient and liking it that way. I've seen how this female image has permeated the American consciousness to the point of influencing everything from the selling of pancakes to the structuring of welfare benefits. But the strangest thing is that when I walked around my neighborhood or went into the homes of family and friends, this matriarch was nowhere to be found.

I know the statistics: They say that when my grandmother was born at the turn of the century as few as 10 percent of black households were headed by females; when I was born at mid-century it had crept to 17 percent; and now it is almost 60 percent. No longer a widow or a divorcee as in times past, the single woman with children today probably has never married — and increasingly she is getting younger. By the time she is 18, one out of every four black unmarried women has become a mother.

But it is a long leap from a matrifocal home, where the father is absent, to a matriarchal one, in which the females take total charge from the males. Though I have known black women heading households in different parts of the country and in different social circumstances — poor, working class or professional — none of them has gloried in the conditions that left them with the emotional and financial responsibility for their families. Often they had to take domestic work because of the flexible hours or stay in menial factory or office jobs because of the steady pay. And leaving the job was only to go home to the other job of raising children alone. These women understood the importance of input from black men in sustaining their families. Their advice and, sometimes, financial assistance were sought and accepted. But if such were not forthcoming, she would continue to deal with her situation alone.

This is a far cry from the heartwarming image of the two-fisted black woman I watched striding across the public imagination. A myth always arises to serve a need. And so it must be asked, what is it in the relationship of black women to American society that has called for them to be seen as independent Amazons?

The black woman was brought to America for the same reason as the black man — to provide slave labor. But she had what seemed to be contradictory roles: She did the woman's work of bearing children and keeping house while doing a man's work at the side of the black male in the fields. She worked regardless of the advanced stages of pregnancy. In the 19th century the ideal of the true woman was one of piety, purity, domesticity and submissiveness; the female lived as a wife sheltered at home or went abroad as a virgin doing good works. But if the prevailing belief was that the natural state of women was one of frailty, how could the black female be explained? Out in the fields laboring with their muscled bodies and during rest periods suckling infants at their breasts, the slave women had to be seen as different from white women. They were stronger creatures: they didn't feel pain in childbirth; they didn't have tear ducts. Ironically, one of the arguments for enslaving blacks in the first place was that as a race they were inferior to whites — but black women, well, they were a little *more* than women.

The need to view slavery as benign accounted for the larger-than-life mammy of the plantation legends. As a house servant, she was always pictured in close proximity to her white masters because there was nothing about her that was threatening to white ideas about black women. Her unstinting devotion assuaged any worries that slaves were discontented or harbored any potential for revolt. Her very dark skin belied any suspicions of past interracial liaisons, while her obesity and advanced age removed any sexual threat. Earth mother, nursemaid and cook, the mammy existed without a history or a future.

In reality, slave women in the house or the field were part of a kinship network and with their men tried to hold together their own precarious families. Marriages between slaves were not legally recognized, but this did not stop them from entering into living arrangements and acting as husbands and wives. After emancipation a deluge of black couples registered their unions under the law, and ex-slaves were known to travel hundreds of miles in search of lost partners and children.

No longer bound, but hardly equal citizens, black men and women had access to only the most menial jobs in society, the largest number being reserved solely for female domestics. Richard Wright wrote a terribly funny and satirical short story about the situation, "Man of All Work." His protagonist is unable to find a job to support his family and save his house from foreclosure, so he puts on his wife's clothes and secures a position as a housekeeper. "Don't stop me. I've found a solution to our problem. I'm an army-trained cook. I can clean a house as good as anybody. Get my point? I put on your dress. I looked in the mirror. I can pass. I want that job."

Pushed to the economic forefront of her home, the 19th century mammy became 20th century Sapphire. Fiery, younger, more aggressive, she just couldn't wait to take the lead away from the man of the house. Whatever he did was never enough. Not that he wanted to do anything, of course, except hang out on street corners, gamble and run around with women. From vaudeville of the 1880s to the advent of *Amos 'n' Andy*, it was easier to make black men the brunt of jokes than to address the inequities that kept decent employment from those who wanted to work. Society had not failed black women — their men had.

The truth is that throughout our history black women could depend upon their men even when they were unemployed or underemployed. But in the impoverished inner cities today we are seeing the rise of the *unemployable*. These young men are not equipped to take responsibility for themselves, much less the children they are creating. And with the increasing youth of unwed mothers, we have grandmothers and grandfathers in their early thirties. How can a grandmother give her daughter's family the traditional wisdom and support when she herself has barely lived? And on the other side of town, where the professional black woman is heading a household, usually because she is divorced, the lack of a traditional kinship network — the core community of parents, uncles, aunts — makes her especially alone.

What is surprising to me is that the myth of the matriarch lives on — even among black women. I've talked to so many who believe that they are supposed to be superhuman and bear up under all things. When they don't, they all too readily look for the fault within themselves. Somehow they failed their history. But it is a grave mistake for black women to believe that they have a natural ability to be stronger than other women. Fifty-seven percent of black homes being headed by females is not natural. A 40 percent pregnancy rate among our young girls is not natural. It is heartbreaking. The myth of the matriarch robs a woman caught in such circumstances of her individuality and her humanity. She should feel that she has the *right* at least to break down — once the kids are put to bed — and do something so simple as cry.

Reading Cyborgs, Writing Feminism: Reading the Body in Contemporary Culture

Anne Balsamo

Research Scientist. Working at Xerox PARC since 1999 as a member of a research group called "RED" whose charge is to do *Research on Experimental Documents.* This includes research and experimentation on the design and prototyping of new document types and new media genres.
Her homepage: http://www.parc.xerox.com/red/members/abalsamo/

Well I stopped in at the body shop
I said to the guy, I want stereo FM
installed in my teeth.
And take this mole off my back
and put it on my cheek.
And while I'm here,
why don't you give me
some of those
high-heeled feet?

Laurie Anderson, "Monkey's Paw"

From Mary Shelley's *Frankenstein*, published in 1818, to Maria, the robot in *Metropolis* (Lang, 1927), to *Frankenhooker* (a film released on video in 1989), the possibilities of human hybrids have fired our cultural imagination as the Western world has developed through the industrial revolution into the age of high technology. But the decade of the 1980s stands out as the historical moment when a high-tech human hybrid moved off the pages of science fiction novels into everyday life: it was in many ways the decade of the cyborg. In 1986, Max Headroom stuttered his way onto American television and the cover of *Newsweek*. That same year Elektra Assassin, Frank Miller's celebrated antihero, challenged the revitalized comic book industry's vision of a proper heroine. By Christmas 1990, it was clear that Transformers™ were the toy of the decade, edging out sales of plastic figures of other popular cyborgs such as RoboCop, Terminator, and Captain Picard's Borg. During the 1993, Christmas season, The Mighty Morphins PowerRangers™ flew off the shelves of U.S.-based *Toys R Us* discount stores; some parent went so far as to bribe toy store workers to find Mighty Mophins™ for their videogame-weary children.

Cyborg, a shorthand term for "cybernetic organism," usually describes a human-machine coupling, most often a *man*-machine hybrid. Cyborgs are alternately labeled "androids," "replicants," or "bionic humans." Whatever label they attract, the cyborg serves not only as the focal figure of the mass-mediated popular culture of American techno-science, but also as the figuration of posthuman identity in postmodernity. From children's plastic action figures to cyberpunk mirrorshades, cyborgian artifacts will endure as relics of an age obsessed with the limits of human mortality and the possibilities of technological replication. In this chapter, I discuss how our technological imagination imbues cyborgs with ancient anxieties about human difference. But first a long detour is in order. I want to revisit the issue of "reading the body" as a way of constructing a framework for "reading cyborgs." This requires a discussion of certain developments within cultural theory, by Michel Foucault, Mary Douglas, and Donna Haraway, as well as other feminists, all of whom contribute to a framework for interpreting the body as a cultural text. This detour is necessary for a second reason. It shows how the female body historically was constructed as a hybrid case, thus making it compatible with notions of cyborg identity promulgated by more recent cultural theorists.

Reading the Body

When the body is said to be "inscribed," "painted," or "written," it makes sense to write of the "discourse of the body," meaning the patterned ways that the body is represented according to broader cultural determinations and also the way that the body becomes a bearer of signs and cultural meaning. Following the work of Michel Foucault, several scholars — including Bryan Turner, Catherine Gallagher and Thomas Laqueur, and Emily Martin, among others — address the relationship between the body, culture, and society to enumerate the ways in which the body is put into discourse. Using a variety of strategies, these scholars study modes of representation of the body: its iconography, its aesthetic and symbolic functions, or its discursive repression. Although they propose different body projects — Turner, for example, is concerned about reconstructing the problem of order as a problem of the government of the body, while Martin presents an ethnographic investigation of women's experiences with reproduction and menstruation — each scholar enacts a reading process that supports the theoretical understanding of the body as a sign-bearing (textual) form. To claim that the body is a discursive construction, and therefore can be read, already effects a deconstruction of its natural posture. Such is the first act of thick perception.

Michel Foucault is not so much interested in the truth of the body as he is in elaborating the apparatus that produces truth effects at the level of the body. His concern is to describe the discursive systems that produce serious truth claims about bodies. Thus, in his genealogical projects he annotates the intelligibility of the body in terms of the discursive, social, and political practices that construct it as an object/subject with meaning. For example, in *The History of Sexuality*, he describes the four central apparatuses of control that mark the transition between a traditional order and one constituted by "scientific biopower": (1) the hysterization of the female body; (2) the construction of homosexuality; (3) the creation of distinctions among infant, child, and adolescent sexualities; and (4) the establishment of a discourse of perversion. These "apparatuses" organize the deployment of power; control is established through the cultural transformation of the meaning of body practices and bodily markers of identity. In short, these apparatuses identify a "conjunction," or what I understand as an "articulation of discursive practices" that produce body knowledges.

Foucault goes on to delineate the *means* by which power is exercised. Central to his work is the assertion that the *means* of the production of discourse include a more ambiguous process of the construction of knowledge claims. For example, the hysterization of the female body, as one way in which scientific biopower is organized and reified, was accomplished through the exercise of new discursive practices (of science, of psychoanalysis), institutionalized social relations (the family under capitalism), and knowledge claims (the medicalization of the female body). This is to say that the meaning of the female body as a "hysterical entity"— a corporeal being susceptible to hysteria — was a meaning constructed through discursive practices, i.e., not only in the discourses of science and medicine, but also through the establishment of social institutions. These institutions, in turn, reproduce specific knowledge claims through the practices established by the profession and as part of the education and socialization of practitioners. Foucault suggests the term "apparatus" and later "technology" to name the process of connection between discursive practices, institutional relations, and material effects that, working together, produce a meaning or a "truth effect" for the human body.

In this sense, an apparatus or "technology" articulates power relations, systems of communication, and productive activities or practices; "articulate" here is used both in the sense of "expressing" that which is already given or operative and in the sense of conjoining or connecting. So, following Foucault's logic, the notion of "technology" describes the workings of a collection of practices that produce specific cultural effects. Technology names the process whereby discursive practices work interdependently with other cultural forces to produce effects at the level of the body. These effects, in turn, become part of an apparatus of control. Foucault goes on to argue that the notion of technology allows for the analysis of power in terms of a number of concrete relations: (1) systems of differentiation, (2) types of objectives, (3) means of bringing power relations into being, (4) forms of institutionalization, and (5) degrees of rationalization — all of which are *rooted* in social networks, language use, and the human body. I find this notion of a technology and his enumeration of concrete relations particularly useful as a framework for investigating the way in which certain taken-for-granted "truths" are, in fact, culturally constructed and eventually institutionalized. This is of course the theory behind his notion of the "technologies of the self" as well as Teresa de Lauretis's notion of the "technologies of gender." It is also, as I noted in the introduction, the basis for my notion of "technologies of the gendered body."

From a feminist point of view, certainly one of the most obvious "truth effects" of the human body in Foucault's analysis is the gendered identity of what he often identifies simply as "docile bodies." As many feminists have argued, Foucault evades direct consideration of gender as an "effect" produced at the level of the body. His broad-sweeping account of the disciplinary practices that produce subjugated bodies neglects to consider gender as an underlying organizing framework for deciphering the disciplined body. Thus, although he can identify the "hysterization of the female body" as one of the apparatuses of control of the body, his grid of analysis fails to consider gender itself as an organized, institutionalized, system of differences that constitutes the individual body and renders it meaningful. In a way that contradicts his analytical intentions to consider the system of differentiations that make the body meaningful, gender often functions for him as a natural given.

If Foucault's project is to deconstruct (in his own fashion) the most commonsensical, taken-for-granted "truths" about the workings of power, it is clear that he runs into problems with his elision of gender. This fact has provoked several feminists to reevaluate the history he offers. For example, in Diamond and Quinby's *Feminism and Foucault* Francis Bartkowski argues quite directly that "what Foucault has done is to reproduce and produce as history the patriarchal history of sexuality." It is clear that throughout his project he treats the gender identity of the female body as a naturally occurring bodily characteristic instead of a "truth effect" produced by cultural discourses that constructs some bodies as active and disciplines others to be passive. Within his analysis, gender materializes as a key "dividing practice" that objectifies the human body and makes it intelligible to him, yet he fails to consider it a technology of power/knowledge in its own right. For all his concern to elaborate systems of power *and* resistance, Foucault ends up writing not so much from a site of resistance but from a site of power — male-centered discourse. Given this, perhaps it is unavoidable that the more radical promise of his project would not be realized by him. Several feminist scholars are doing what he could not — articulating a history of sexuality from a site of resistance by addressing the construction of the feminine, femininity, and Woman to describe how gender is, in Foucault's terms, a primary apparatus of scientific biopower that constructs the body as an intelligible object.

For example, in Susan Suleiman's collection of essays *The Female Body in Western Culture* several scholars implicitly rebuke Foucault's oversight by showing how gender is one of the primary effects of the discursive construction of the human body. Suleiman herself poses the question of the female body this way: "what place has the female body occupied in the Western imagination, and in the symbolic productions of Western culture over the past two thousand years?" (I). Foucault would have us believe that "she" was hardly present, marginal and uninteresting at best. The authors in Suleiman's collection collectively argue the contrary; they examine the many different sites of the ideological inscription of sexual difference by looking at representations of the female body in different cultural texts. The essays are organized thematically rather than historically, on the topics of eros, death, mothers, illness, images, and difference. The primary purpose of Suleiman's collection is to argue that the female body is not an essentially unchanging, given-in-nature, biological entity, but rather is symbolically constructed within different cultural discourses situated within different historical conjunctions.

Following Foucault, Suleiman underscores the importance of reading the body as a symbolic *discursive* construction:

> The cultural significance of the female body is not only (not even first and foremost) that of a flesh-and-blood entity, but that of a *symbolic construct*. Everything we know about the body — certainly as regards the past, and even, it could be argued, as regards the present — exists for us in some form of discourse: and discourse, whether verbal or visual, fictive or historical or speculative, is never unmediated, never free of interpretation, never innocent. (2)

The analyses offered in Suleiman's book are textually grounded and politically motivated; taken together, they articulate an understanding of how the relation between the body and culture is mediated through discourse such that the body is transformed into an epistemological issue — knowledge about the body becomes a matter of *representation* of the body. The critical point Suleiman stresses is that there is no "natural" approach to the female body that is rooted in an essentialist female nature. All understandings of the body are mediated through representations which, in turn, are constructed through interpretive frameworks. This approach, like

Foucault's, keeps the body contained within discourse and subject(ed) to determinate systems of power and knowledge. But in many respects, this collection skirts the dangerous line of suggesting that knowledge of the body is *only* discursive. Or, put another way, when Suleiman writes that the "cultural significance" of the body is a matter of its symbolic construction, not its "natural femininity," she comes close to asserting that this is the singular definition of the female body. This approach *inadvertently* ends up invoking a dualistic logic, that the female body is either a "flesh and blood entity" or a symbolic construct. I stress the term "inadvertently" to remind readers of the historical situation of the production of this approach to the study of the female body. It was an approach that sought to correct the overreliance on an essentialist definition of the female body as a biological or "natural" entity. Since that time, feminist discussions of the constitution of the female body have been often sidelined by *debates* about the effectivity of essentialist versus anti-essentialist perspectives. I would like to sidestep this debate by focusing attention on the ways in which nature and culture are mutually determining systems of understanding. While it is true, as Suleiman says, that "everything we know about the body . . . exists for us in some form of discourse," this discourse is not entirely divorced from the material manifestation of the "flesh and blood" entity.

Building on the work of Marcel Mauss, cultural anthropologist Mary Douglas describes the relationship between symbolic systems, social structures, and the body by analyzing the way cultural systems rely on the body's expressive resources to formulate social relations. In her book *Natural Symbols*, Douglas asserts that social perceptions of the human body are never free from determining cultural influences; the body is always comprehended as an interaction between the materiality of what is given in a particular body and the symbolic constructions of the "body" embedded within a given culture. But the most important point she makes is that although the meaning of the *physical body* is itself structured by the symbolic representation of the body, it is at the same time an experiential resource for the construction of such representations:

> The social body constrains the way the physical body is perceived. The physical experience of the body, always modified by the social categories through which it is known, sustains a particular view of society. There is a continual exchange of meanings between the two kinds of bodily experience so that each reinforces the categories of the other. (65)

In this statement, Douglas follows Mauss by asserting that the human body is *always* defined according to cultural beliefs about social relations. But even as Douglas asserts that "most symbolic behavior must work through the body" (vii), she argues that the *meaning* of the body, and thus the meaning of different systems of body symbols, is, in fact, constructed through "a continual exchange of meanings between *two* kinds of bodily experience" (65) — of the physical body and of the social (or symbolic) body. While I don't want to belabor the point, it is important to note that Douglas keeps the notion of the physical body at the heart of her account of the cultural construction of the symbolic body. Her broader point, of course, is to argue that although the physical body is in many ways a naturally occurring referent for symbolic systems, its meaning is not "naturally" determined (vii). In this sense, there are no natural symbols, although there are plentiful symbolic representations of nature and of the "natural body."

Douglas offers an important contribution to an understanding of the cultural construction of the gendered body. "There can be no natural way of considering the body," she writes, "that does not involve at the same time a social dimension." This assertion denaturalizes both the body and gender and provides a basis for accomplishing what Brown and Adams identify as a critical feminist project — the deconstruction of the "natural" female body. Following this, gender identity can be redefined as a body attribute that is assigned, organized, and acquired through the process of social perception; in short, it can no longer be considered a "natural fact" of the human body. Rather, we must consider how the human body is "gendered" through a series of social acts that often begin long before physical birth and are determined only partially by personal (self-decipherment) perception of physiological body parts (the genitals, for example). But the important issue here is not only that gender is "denaturalized" but that so too are definitions of gender that rely on appeals to the natural body. Behind the construction of representations of "natural bodies" and "natural" gender identities, Douglas claims are beliefs and anxieties about the social body.

In keeping with Douglas's line of analysis, Thomas Laqueur argues that the female body was at the center of a radical 18th-century reinterpretaion of the patriarchal social hierarchy. Sexual difference was reconsidered such that the female body was no longer considered merely an inferior, underdeveloped, and infantile version of the male body (ovaries as underdeveloped testicles, for example); rather a complementary relation between the male and female body was established, such that

> [w]riters of all sorts were determined to base what they insisted were fundamental differences between male and female sexuality, and thus between man and woman, on discoverable biological distinctions . . . . Thus the old model, in which men and women were arrayed according to their degree of metaphysical perfection, their vital heat, along an axis whose telos was male, gave way by the late 18th century to a new model of difference, of biological divergence. An anatomy and physiology of incommensurability replaced a metaphysics of hierarchy in the representation of women in relation to men.

Since Laqueur explicitly draws on Douglas in his analysis of the construction of the female body, it is not surprising that he situates this transformation of the cultural understanding of the "nature" of the female body within the changing constitution of the 18th-century social order, "when the basis for a new order of sex and gender became a critical issue of political theory and practice"(4). Laqueur points out that the new order (which replaced the divine right of kings, a similar point of analysis in Foucault's historical genealogy) was concerned to establish naturalized hierarchies among human bodies. He explains how such a cultural imperative and the use of metaphors (of heat, of oestrus) functioned to define the female body in terms of its reproductive biology. The hierarchical relation between the male body and the female body was not overturned; rather

> the political, economic and cultural transformations of the 18th century created the context in which the articulation of radical differences between the sexes became culturally imperative. In a world in which science was increasingly viewed as providing insight into the fundamental truths of creation, in which nature as manifested in the unassailable reality of bones and organs was taken to be the only foundation of the moral order, a biology of incommensurability became the means by which such differences could be authoritatively represented. (35)

Here Laqueur offers an account of the exercise of scientific biopower on the female body. The turn toward a biologically based definition of the complementarity of the female body raised new questions about the relationship between that body and social control. For if female bodies are fundamentally different from male bodies, not just an inferior version, the issue of control becomes more critical: how does one control a body that isn't entirely knowable?

In her examination of medical textbooks of the nineteenth century, Mary Poovey illuminates the historical construction of the female body as the object of medical attention and control. Moreover, she explicates how medical discourse constructed the female body as excessive and threatening to the epistemological boundaries of the prevailing social order. Specifically she focuses on the medical debates concerning forms of anesthesia to show how they function as a discursive site of the struggle for authority over the female body between obstetricians, midwives, and other medical practitioners. Not incidentally it is a site in which the female body is thoroughly silent/silenced:

> [t]he debate presented itself as an argument about the nature of women and medicine's proper relation to them . . . . First, does the woman in labor properly belong to the realm of nature, which is governed by God, or to culture, where nature submits to man? Second, how can a man know — so as to master — the female body, which is always other to his own?

If the female body properly belonged to nature, the argument went, then midwives were better positioned to serve the laboring maternal body, being female bodies themselves and skilled in reading the natural labor signs of that body. If the female body could be secured as belonging to the cultural order, then, by extension, it was beholden to the cultural authority of medicine and medical discourse and would be properly served by the administration of chloroform during labor (one of the two forms of anesthesia being debated).

At this point, Poovey implies that the articulation among new technologies (forms of anesthesia), social debates about medical authority and the status of medicine as a scientifically rational practice, and a definition of the female body as governed by its reproductive capacity, establishes a definition of the female body as "always lacking and needing control":

> This set of assumptions — that woman's reproductive function defines her character, position, and value, that this function is only one sign of an innate periodicity, and that this biological periodicity influences and is influenced by an array of nervous disorders — mandates the medical profession's superintendence of women . . . . [quoting Dr. Issac Ray:] With women, it is but a step from extreme nervous susceptibility to downright hysteria, and from that to overt insanity . . . . Seen in this way, hysteria is simultaneously the norm of the female body taken to its logical extreme and a medical category that effectively defines this norm as inherently abnormal. (146-47)

Furthermore, Poovey explains:

> On the one hand, representing woman as an inherently unstable female body authorizes ceaseless medical monitoring and control. But on the other hand, this representation of woman as always requiring control produces her as always already exceeding the control that medicine can exercise. (147)

Consequently, the female body is defined as simultaneously belonging within the "proper" domain of medical discourse and yet always threatening its epistemological boundaries. Here we read the conflation between the political contest to establish the physiological facts of female nature, and the physiological consequences of symbolic representations of the female body.

The female body that is an effect of the construction of identity/

authority of obstetricians in nineteenth-century medical discourse is a hybrid creature formed through the articulations among social practices, the development of new knowledge, and changing patterns of power and authority. In this sense, the female body functions as a border case; it is at once defined as part of a natural order *and* as an intensely fascinating and yet threatening object of cultural control. Its excessiveness strains the cultural authority of medical knowledge. As such it is a site of potential transgression against the boundaries of social order, at once constituted within the dominant discourses of science and medicine but threatening to the epistemological certainty of that discourse.

Panic Postmodernism and the Disappearing Body

The story about the female body doesn't change much in more recent history, especially in cultural narratives of postmodern identity. In *Body Invaders*, a collection of essays on panic sex in America, editor Arthur Kroker also seeks to intervene in the reproduction of a dominant discourse of the body that would define it as an organic, natural entity. Following Marshall McLuhan, Kroker argues that the "natural" body has disappeared, replaced by a technologically produced simulacrum. Kroker reads the current list of "panic" *body* issues (AIDS, anorexia, addictions of all sorts) as signs of significant *social* anxieties concerning control and safety. The "panic body" marks "a declining culture where the body is revived, and given one last burst of hyper-subjectivity, as the inscribed text for all the stress and crisis-symptoms of the death of the social" (27). With this statement he reasserts Douglas's understanding that "cultures think themselves through the body." He sees the proliferation of rhetorics that work feverishly to invest the body with meaning as a symptom of a culture in decline — a culture where meaning has been banished. For Kroker the body is simply obsolete, replaced by numerous technological extensions of its senses. The prevalence of body rhetorics masks the disappearance of the natural body (now replaced by technological devices) which in turn, masks the disappearance of the social — the final death of social solidarity that comes from daily living with the apocalypse. Discourse, now objectified as communication technologies, literally replaces the material body with simulated body senses. Whereas Foucault's project was to explicate how the discourses of modernity redefined the body as machine, in postmodernity what we discover is that technology now transforms the body into nothing more than discourse.

With the disappearance of the material body in McLuhan's analysis of media culture and Kroker's reading of postmodernity, gender too presumably becomes ephemeral, or at best an artifact of an outdated rhetoric that seeks to invest the body with meaning. And yet, we can read in both McLuhan's and Kroker's analyses a submerged discourse of gender that continues to organize and make intelligible the discourses of the body in late capitalism. Even as he claims that the velocity of cultural change blurs the boundaries upon which identity is constructed, Kroker identifies the special status of the female body in postmodernity:

> Because now as ever, the play of power within and against the text of women's bodies is an early warning sign of a grisly power field that speaks the language of body invaders. As privileged objects of a domination that takes as its focus the inscription of the text of the body, women have always known the meaning of a relational power that works in the language of body invaders. This is not, though, the wager of an old patriarchal power that announces itself in the transcendent and externalized language of hierarchy, univocity, and logocentricity, but a power field that can be multiple, pleasurable, and indeed, fully embodied . . . . women's bodies have always been postmodern because they have always been targets of a power which, inscribing the text of the flesh, seeks to make of feminine identity something interpellated by ideology, constituted by language, and the site of a "dissociated ego." (24)

Kroker elaborates this language of body invaders as the conspicuous consumption of late capitalism, which turns all bodies into sign vehicles for fetishistic commodities. As a companion to McLuhan's "Mechanical Bride," "The Capezio Woman" figures as a final icon in Kroker's analysis. Whereas the Mechanical Bride symbolizes the female body of American media culture that is docile, traditional, and subjected to "the wager of old patriarchal power," the Capezio Woman symbolizes the female body that is stylish, pleasure-anointed, and happy to find a snappy pair of new shoes. Both images testify to the persistence (nonobsolescence) of gender in a postcorporeal world. Even when the body is reduced to a discursive effect, notes Kroker, the female body functions as the privileged sign of the "body debased, humiliated, and inscribed to excess by all the signs of consumer culture"(33).

Upon closer reading, the female body hasn't been transformed at all; it is still *constructed* as the message-bearing and silent form of the (eighteenth and nineteenth centuries') unruly body, produced through the formation of the cultural imaginary; only now the cultural imaginary is expressed through the rhetoric of "panic" postmodernism. The female body continues to function as the sign of a gendered body opposed to a nonmarked (human) body that is said to be *now* (in late capitalism) subjugated to discursive systems of power and knowledge. If women have *always* been postmodern bodies, as Kroker asserts, then what is different about postmodern bodies that hasn't always been the condition of female bodies? The *compulsion* to theorize the condition of postmodern bodies as something new or even exhausted is due to the novelty the male body experiences coming under this totalizing system for the first time; understandably, panic results. In Kroker's analysis, female bodies continue to mark gender; thus they announce the deployment of a gendered opposition of bodies in postmodern theory. This is a gendered opposition, whereby the One (recently "invaded" body) is unmarked by gender and the Other (the always postmodern body) is female. Such is the fate of the female body in the postmodern cultural imaginary: an always silent/silenced conceptual placeholder in hysterical male discourse. As before, her excessiveness threatens the very order of the system.

Is it ironic that the body disappears in postmodern theory just as women and feminists have emerged as an intellectual force within the human disciplines? A similar (ironic?) contradiction emerges with respect to the issue of the body. An organic body *marked* by certain biological characteristics provided a common identity for women to collectivize as feminists. But the bodily identity of woman proved unstable and unreliable as a source of collective empowerment. Diverse feminist action directs its attention to de-essentializing the biological identity of woman, thus working to deconstruct the organic foundation of feminist thought. After acknowledging the impossibility of biological essentialism as a foundation for the identity of "woman," feminist thinking proceeds to an analysis of the cultural construction of the body, and is immediately confronted with a discourse that gleefully joins it in deconstructing biological essentialism. In the process, feminists encounter unsolicited assistance in doing away with "the body," which served — at one point, if not now — as the necessary foundation of women's empowerment.

Faced with the prospect of being strategically eclipsed within the modern episteme once again, feminists have a political stake in constructing and critiquing theories of the body within postmodernism. As I have argued elsewhere, it is time for feminism to crash the postmodern party. The final fate of "the body" should not be left entirely to the panic postmodernists — that is, Jean Baudrillard, Deleuze and Guattari, among others. Moreover, we cannot listen obediently while these very same postmodernists delineate for us "the special place of feminist theory today" and lay out for us the proper attitude that feminism should adopt toward the body. But what is a feminist to do?

In her book *Gynesis: Configurations of Woman and Modernity*, Alice Jardine cautions feminist writers: "The attempt to analyze, to separate ideological and cultural determinations of the 'feminine' from the 'real woman' — seemingly the most logical path for a feminist to follow — may also be the most interminable process, one in which women become not only figuratively but also literally impossible." Jardine describes the paradoxical situation of feminist criticism that on the one hand draws political strength from an essentialist identity of "woman," but on the other has been convinced of the necessity to interrogate such an identity for the differences it obscures:

> While proceeding from a "belief" (in women's oppression), we are nevertheless, necessarily, caught up in a permanent whirlwind of reading practices within a universe of fiction and theory written, but for a few official exceptions, by men. Not believing in "Truth," we continue to be fascinated by (elaborate) fictions. This is the profound paradox of the feminist speaking in our contemporary culture: she proceeds from a *belief* in a world from which — even the philosophers admit — Truth has disappeared. This paradox, it seems to me, can lead to (at least) three possible scenarios: a renewed silence, a form of religion (from of mysticism to political orthodoxy), or a continual attention — historical, ideological, and affective — to the place from which we speak. (31-32)

Another possible solution is to reconstruct our reading practices — which is ultimately what Jardine advocates. She suggests that feminists begin to write new fictions, written through "the continual attention — historical, ideological, and affective — to the place from which we speak" (32). This, to me, perfectly describes Donna Haraway's response to feminism's "profound paradox," and indeed, the founding imperative for her feminist manifesto; in elaborating a new fiction of feminist identity, her "ironic political myth" of cyborg citizenship, she enacts a new reading practice that takes the discursively constructed material body as its starting point and narrates a reconstructed fiction of gender identity.

Reading Cyborgs

According to Haraway, in "A Manifesto for Cyborgs," the only bodies that stand a chance in postmodern culture are cyborg bodies. Cyborg bodies are constructed by communication networks and other hybrid discourses such as biotechnology, biopolitics, and female bodybuilding. Variously used as a symbol of antitechnological sentiments or of the possibilities of "better living through chemistry," cyborgs are a product of fears and desires that run deep within our cultural imaginary. Through the use of technology as the means or context for human hybridization, cyborgs come to represent unfamiliar "otherness," one that challenges the denotative stability of human identity. Andreas Huyssen claims that the crisis of modernism pivots on the problematic of otherness. In this way, cyborgs offer a particularly appropriate emblem of postmodern identity, since cyborg identity is predicated on transgressed boundaries. They fascinate us because they are not like us and yet are just like us. Formed through a radical disruption of otherness, cyborg identity foregrounds the constructedness of otherness. Cyborgs alert us to the way in which identity depends on notions of "the other" that are arbitrary, shifting, and ultimately unstable.

Every cyborg image constructs an implicit opposition between machine and human, at once repressing similarities and highlighting distincions. In this way it defines the meaning of both the term "human" and the term "artificial." Signs of humanness and, alternatively, signs of machineness function not only as markers of the "essences" of the dual natures of the hybrid, but also as signs of the inviolable opposition between humans and machines. But because the cyborg embodies both "natures" simultaneously, the resulting hybrid is neither purely human nor purely machine. The distribution of its dual dispositions is never simply symmetrical, and the proximity of each to the other and the combination of dissimilar parts produces a hybrid often unrecognizable as any familiar personage. By disrupting the stable meanings of the human/machine dualism, other reliable oppositions are also rendered unstable. The cyborg, for Haraway, has the potential to disrupt the persistent dualisms that have been "systemic to the logics and practices of domination of women, people of color, nature, workers, animals." The most troublesome dualism include some aleady mentioned in this chapter: culture/nature, human/artificial, male/female, as well as others such as reality/appearance, truth/illusion, theory/politics. Cyborg bodies, then, cannot be conceived as belonging wholly to either culture or nature; they are neither wholly technological nor completely organic. In a similar sense, cyborg bodies cannot be completely discursive. Cyborgs are a matter of fiction and a matter of lived experience. They not only subvert the certainty of what counts as nature, but, as Haraway lays out, they also subvert the certainty of the "textualization of everything" by pointing to the lived relations of domination that ground cultural reading(s).

By reasserting a material body, the cyborg rebukes the disappearance of the body within postmodernism. Yet it never contradicts the variety of discurrsive constructions of the female body. The cyborg connects a discursive body with a historically material body by taking account of the ways in which the body is constructed within different social and cultural formations. Ultimately, the cyborg challenges feminism to search for ways to study the body as it is at once both a cultural construction and a material fact of human life. The impact of this is decisive: understanding that the body is culturally, not "naturally," constructed means that the body is not solely a matter of materiality; nor can it be reductively a matter of discourse. Its "nature" is culturally determined even when this nature is said to be discursively constructed. To claim that the body is a discursive as well as material construction still leaves everything to say about the particular cultural design of that body within any given historical conjunction.

Haraway explicitly maps the identity of woman onto the image of the cyborg. This foregrounds the ambiguous constitution of the female body — predicated on the blurred boundaries between the individual and the collective, the material and the discursive, the fictive and the real. Both Woman and Cyborg are simultaneously symbolically and biologically produced and reproduced through social interactions. The "self" is one interactional product; the body is another. The cyborg further displaces the nature-versus-culture opposition since it is clear in this age of body technologies that the givenness of the female body is a constructed artifact of various systems of meaning. Moreover, as Haraway reminds us, the search for a female "nature" is a utopian quest, which threatens to distract contemporary feminists from more important tasks, such as forming coalitions and alliances with other political groups based not on some natural gender identification, but on the necessity for shared political strategies. This tactical plan of action depends upon feminism's willingness to investigate how women live permanently partial identities, to discover what cultural meanings are taken up, how they are resisted, and in the process, ultimately transformed.